D0875761

What Unemployment Means

What
Unemployment
Means

ADRIAN SINFIELD

MARTIN ROBERTSON · OXFORD

First published in 1981 by Martin Robertson, Oxford

British Library Cataloguing in Publication Data

Sinfield, Adrian
  What unemployment means.
  1. Labor supply – Great Britain
  I. Title
  331.13'7941   HD5765.A6
ISBN 0-85520-406-0 Pbk

Typeset by Cambrian Typesetters, Farnborough, Hants.
printed and bound in Great Britain
by Billing and Sons Limited
Guildford, London, Oxford, Worcester

Contents

INTRODUCTION   The End of Full Employment?   1

Chapter 1   The Unemployed   7
      1.1   How Many Are Out of Work?   7
      1.2   The Unequal Burden of Unemployment   18
      1.3   The Geography of Unemployment   23
      1.4   Let them move to work?   28

Chapter 2   Being Out of Work   35
      2.1   The Experience of Unemployment   35
      2.2   The Search for Work   41
      2.3   The Organisation of the Unemployed   47
      2.4   Poverty Out of Work   49

Chapter 3   Who are the Unemployed?   58
      3.1   Mass Redundancies in a Cold Climate   58
      3.2   Youth Without Work   68
      3.3   The Disposable Older Worker   76
      3.4   Women Unemployed   83
      3.5   The Long-term Unemployed   89

Chapter 4   Services for the Unemployed   97
      4.1   The Employment Service After the Cuts   97
      4.2   Social Security and Economic Insecurity   106

Chapter 5   The Wider Impact   119
      5.1   A Jobless Society   119
      5.2   Equal Opportunity Without Work?   122
      5.3   The Meaning of Full Employment   127

Chapter 6   The Micro-Chip and the Economy   133
        6.1   The Micro-Electronic Revolution   133
        6.2   Unemployment and the Economy   140

Chapter 7   Work for All   147

Bibliography   158

Index   165

TABLES

1 Unemployment Rates Adjusted to US Concepts,
   1960--1980   14
2 Male Unemployment Rates by Duration for each
   Region, October 1980   24
3 Cheapest Family Homes in Watford and North
   Shields newspapers, December 1980   30

FIGURES

1 Unemployed and Vacancies in the United Kingdom
   1963—80   8
2 Unemployment by Region, November 1980 and
   1979   25

Preface

The apparently wide general acquiescence in higher un-employment provided the stimulus to write this book. The push came from Michael Hay and Sue Corbett at Martin Robertson: they were provoked by the announcement of two million unemployed to challenge me to attempt a short account of the meaning of unemployment in Britain today and provided help and support throughout the enterprise.

Many other people gave me valuable guidance, assistance and encouragement, and I am particularly grateful to Tony Atkinson, Alan Deacon, Trevor Davies, John Foster, Dan Finn, Neil Fraser, Jean Hartley, Michael Hill, Joe Kenyon, Clarissa and Tim Notley, Chris Pond, Jennie Popay, Lindsey Rhodes, Connie Sorrentino, John Veit-Wilson, Alan Walker and Hans Wirz.

Special thanks are due to Valerie Chuter who enabled me to keep to a rashly-accepted timetable by the efficient and unruffled speed with which she produced typescript from much amended manuscript and dictation; to Liz Paton who constructively applied all the skills of copy-editing with great patience and enthusiasm over Christmas; and to Dorothy Sinfield whose hard work as unpaid editor, critic and research assistant made her constant support all the more valuable and vital.

Adrian Sinfield
December 1980

We so soon become used to the thought of want that we do not feel that an evil which grows greater to the sufferer the longer it lasts becomes less to the observer by the very fact of its duration.

ALEXIS DE TOCQUEVILLE

INTRODUCTION—
The End of Full Employment?

In August 1980 unemployment in the United Kingdom reached 2 million in the official figures. Since then the total has risen even faster: no one is predicting any significant reduction in 1981, and most forecasters expect the numbers out of work to grow and remain very high throughout the decade. Even those who foresee an improvement in the economy and a reduction in inflation offer no hope of a decline in unemployment with present policies. Others draw attention to changes they see occurring very largely outside governments' control that will maintain high unemployment and increase it further still. The collapse of work is now seen by an increasing number of people as a sombre and by no means far-fetched or hysterical forecast for the next decade.

From the deepening gloom has emerged a consensus that the days of 'full employment' are not only over; they are now as much a part of social history, which we may regard with nostalgia or contempt according to taste, as hoolahoops and spats. Whatever the disputes and conflicts among those expecting the permanent change to higher unemployment, this belief has become much stronger during the last few years. It is part of the reality that must be accepted as we attempt to tackle the major economic, social, political and industrial problems facing Britain in the last two decades of the twentieth century.

There are many arguments put forward to support this view. All tend to point to the inevitability and/or desirability of the abandonment of full employment as an objective of economic policy and a goal for society. Varying weight is

1

given to different reasons but among the main ones are the following six.

(1)   The long-term impact of the world recession and the dramatic growth in economic and political power of the oil-producing countries of the Middle East. There are some 7 million out of work in the European Community and unemployment has been rising in many other industrial societies. The calculation of unemployment is more difficult in Third World countries, with large rural populations trying to maintain an existence from the land, but well over 300 million people are without any form of regular work.

(2)   The specific changes within Britain resulting from major and prolonged economic and industrial problems. They include the long-term decline in our share of world markets with our decreasing competitiveness, inadequate increases in productivity and excessive levels of inflation — and the failures of successive governments in their economic policies and industrial strategies to make any impact on these problems. Whether the achievements of undeviating Tory monetarism will bring us to a 'brave new world' or simply convert a cyclical recession into a chronic slump, we are already being encouraged not only to expect, but to accept, current and even higher levels of unemployment.

(3)   The coming crisis of the micro-electronic revolution. This will hit Britain most severely just as the advantages of North Sea oil are flowing away and will dramatically reduce the need for workers, let alone absorb any of the unemployed.

(4)   The labour force will continue to be swollen by more young and inexperienced school leavers and by the return to work of more married women. These are both groups with a traditionally higher level of unemployment, and one must expect this vulnerability to increase with our diminishing capacity to create new jobs.

(5)   A new vigour to the critique of employment and the work ethic. This is coming from many directions and takes many forms. Supporters of the new technology draw

attention to its potential for increasing the opportunity for leisure. Others point to the drudgery and toil of many jobs, the inadequacy of the reward and the triviality of the products. There is renewed criticism and rejection of a society that measures worth by the work that you do and not by the sort of person you are. Some at least see an opportunity to counter this as the amount of work to be done diminishes and believe the years of full employment helped to reinforce the class-ridden dominance of the work ethic.

(6) A women's movement that emphasises how much vital work is neglected and given no recognition. In particular, the unpaid labour in the home, which is carried out predominantly by women, is both taken for granted and undervalued. We also continue to assess the status of a whole family by what the husband does and deny any real equality to women. Some believe that full employment was for men only and reinforced the gulf between home and work; others that it created or reinforced the dual careers of paid employment and unpaid housework that lay an unequal burden on women.

The cumulative weight of these points, however caricatured by brief summary here, has led to a remarkable consensus. We are moving into a new world as distant from the 1950s and 1960s as these decades appear to be from the 1920s and 1930s. Many believe that we are going back to the wasted years of the thirties; but this time there can be no war from which we may emerge into a state of higher welfare and fuller employment, even at the terrible cost paid from 1939 to 1945.

Acceptance of the abandonment of full employment brings together very strange bedfellows. Radical critics, welcoming a decline in the work ethic, jostle with employers expecting the iron discipline of unemployment to control workers and their unions. Women struggling to escape the long-established inequalities that lock them into the monotony of housework and deny them equal opportunity outside the home encounter re-emerging traditionalists who hope that the lack of work will force mothers to stay at home and carry out their 'proper' tasks, with an end to the scandal of latch-key children. Those who believe that new technologies will allow more to be produced with less toil and more pleasantly in small community enterprises face many trade unionists committed to defending the jobs of their members and employers who expect a glut of labour to reduce wage demands and restrictive practices and permit them to run their factories properly.

There is no reason to deny the validity of any view simply because others share it for very different reasons. But it should perhaps give us pause that such varying reasons should be accepted without clearer recognition of the conflicts. Nevertheless the shared message is clear: except for the occasional Luddite spasms of a trade union movement under attack, full employment is now off the political agenda.

The purpose of this book is to register a dissent from what is coming to be the prevailing wisdom. The achievement of full employment was too easily and uncritically accepted in the two decades following the end of the war. Now I believe that this objective is being equally easily and uncritically abandoned. Our complacent failure to recognise the need to maintain the struggle to achieve full employment has left us far too vulnerable to the cries for its abandonment. The essentially conservative nature of my argument should be underlined. Despite our sceptical posture at all times, social scientists have been just as prone as other members of society to anticipate and exaggerate change. We may like to see ourselves sitting in the cockpit and acting as 'the radar of society'. But in fact we have a better, though not particularly good, record of sitting in the back seat, gazing in the rear-view mirror and discovering where we have been rather than where we are going.

Evidence of how quickly assumptions change is provided by contrasting the early 1980s with the early 1960s in Britain and the United States. During my first interviews with unemployed families in the north-east of England in late 1963, it was confidently believed by very many people that full employment was established, apart from the occasional hiccup as in the winter of 1962–3, or the occasional pocket of local unemployment. Any value that there was in my research would be in its contribution to social history rather than to the analysis and making of contemporary social policy. When I went to carry out similar research in upstate New York the following year, I was surprised to discover that the very much higher levels of American unemployment were expected to continue rising — the opposite assumption from that prevailing in low-unemployment Britain. Fears of the computer-led technological revolution were sharpened by anxieties about severe structural unemployment in the traditional heavy-manufacturing states and the persisting, but then more recognised, inequalities between black and white and rich and poor.

Today, unemployment in Britain is actually higher than in the United States, when the statistics are worked out on the same basis. There appears to be much greater concern in the United States about the level of unemployment but more optimism about bringing it down below current levels. The United States may be lulled by its previous over-reaction to the computer changes, but the general level of debate and anxiety over the potential impact of the micro-electronic revolution is said to be much less than in Britain. This may be because greater use has already been made of the new technology. Most surprisingly, given the British tendency to dismiss the low-unemployment years as a past and once-only departure from the norm, the argument for full employment still appears to be alive in the United States. It may possibly be gathering some wider interest with the debates and passing of the Humphrey-Hawkins Full Employment and Balanced Growth Act in 1978. The National Committee for Full Employment set up in June 1974 has survived as the Full Employment Action Council (see for example Levison, 1980, Ch. 5).

This book attempts to set out the basic findings of research on the unemployed in recent years and to link this to the wider debate about the type of society in which we wish to live. Most of our discussion about the meaning of unemployment has been caught up in various fixed debates little changed since the nineteenth century, let alone the 1930s. How much hardship accompanies unemployment? To what extent are incentives to search for and stay in work weakened by current benefits? How hard are the unemployed really looking for work? These issues still dominate the discussion although their form may have changed.

But there are other questions which need to be answered as well if the abandonment of full employment as a societal goal is to be a conscious decision, and not just a feeble acquiescence that renders inevitable whatever is perceived as such. What is the significance of increased unemployment — both for those who are directly affected and the whole society? What are the short-term and long-term costs; how equally are these distributed across the social structure; and how far are they compensated or borne privately by the individual and family? What are the implications for the achievement of other goals? How does increased unemployment affect the lives of those who remain in work and other members of society?

The first three chapters examine the experience of unemployment in Britain today. They describe the scale of the problem and its distribution across the population; what it is like to be out of work; and how this experience varies among some of the main groups of unemployed. Chapter 4 considers the main services and how effectively they are meeting the needs of people out of work. The significance of high unemployment for the wider society and the social meaning of full employment are discussed in chapter 5. The arguments that technological change and the working of the economy make higher unemployment inescapable are considered in chapter 6, together with the economic costs that increased unemployment creates now and for the future. The final chapter emphasises the main themes of the analysis throughout the book and argues that society's indifference to the problem of unemployment must be challenged.

CHAPTER ONE

The Unemployed

Any analysis of the nature of unemployment today must give an account of how many and who are unemployed. This chapter therefore has to be more statistical than the rest in providing a basis for examining the experience and impact of unemployment. But it also begins to tackle some of the more common misconceptions of the extent and nature of unemployment. The final sections describe the very different distribution of unemployment throughout the United Kingdom and the question of moving to find work.

1.1 HOW MANY ARE OUT OF WORK?

In November 1980 the 2,162,874 people on the official register of the unemployed represented an unemployment rate of 8.9 per cent. This meant almost one in eleven workers had no job, and by the end of the winter the proportion is expected to exceed one in ten. The rate of increase has been dramatic (see Figure 1). For the first twenty years after the war unemployment averaged less than 2 per cent – about 400,000 people out of work compared with over two million today. One million was first reached in the early 1970s, but the expansionary boom of the Conservative government helped to bring the total back down to half a million. During the first three years of the Labour administration it rose again to a new post-war peak in the winter of 1977–78. By then the numbers out of work had increased nearly fourfold in ten years. A new decline was arrested in mid-1979 and from autumn 1979 onwards the figures began to climb with increasing speed.

Figure 1 Unemployed and vacancies in the United Kingdom 1963–80.
Three-month moving average: seasonally adjusted

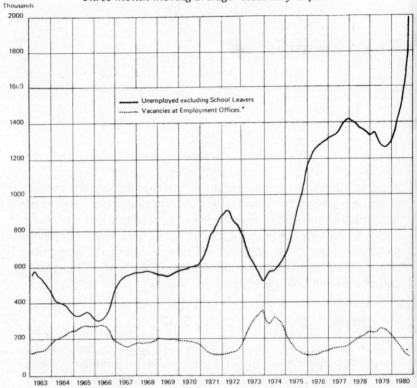

*Vacancies at employment offices are only about a third of total vacancies
Source: Department of Employment Press Notice, 25 November 1980

Two million unemployed in August 1980 was well in advance of the predictions of many denounced as Cassandras in the mid-1970s, and the number has continued to grow. The figures are generally agreed to provide the best indication of the underlying trend, when school leavers are excluded and they are adjusted for seasonal variation. On this basis the monthly increases have been rising sharply with over 100,000 added in October 1980 and another 136,000 in November. The harsh deterioration in unemployment since the mid-1970s is shown by comparing the *lowest* point that unemployment has fallen to recently with the *highest* levels of unemployment in the 1950s and 1960s. The low of autumn 1979 was well over twice as high as any of the peaks in the unemployment figures in the two decades before 1970. Since September 1979 the numbers out of work have increased dramatically. The present point on what is generally agreed to be a rising trend is already over three and a half times above the highest point reached during the 1950s and 1960s. Yet the Prime Minister's declaration to the Conservative Party Conference in October 1980 'You turn: this lady's not for turning' retained a great deal of support at the end of the year, and there has been very little sign of sustained protest. The only big demonstration was held far from London in Merseyside in late November and the speeches of the Labour speakers generally concentrated on denouncing 'Tory unemployment' with surprisingly little reference to any alternative strategy towards long term employment policies. The afternoon given to the discussion of unemployment during the debate on the Queen's Speech in the House of Commons earlier the same week was, with the exception of some lively debate on training, a lacklustre event with the parties trying to blame each other rather than put forward constructive proposals: there was little discussion of any attempt to build an overall strategy to maintain significantly lower unemployment.

The reasons for the lack of any major and widespread protest comparable to those during the interwar years are complex and related to major changes in society that tend to isolate the unemployed from those in work, and so dull our recognition of the impact and meaning of unemployment. There is much support for the views that there are plenty of jobs available; that many people are not really unemployed or are completely unemployable; that the multiple and generous benefits of 'the welfare state' take the sting out of unemployment; and that the growth of an irregular or informal economy provides further resources to the unemployed through the rewards of work on the side. These points are examined in the course of the book, and the first is taken up here. There are many who believe that the jobs are there, but how many jobs are available?

How Many Jobs?

While the total of officially registered unemployed rose by
three-fifths over the twelve months from November 1979,
the number of job vacancies known to employment offices
in the United Kingdom fell by exactly the same proportion.
The total at the end of 1980 (seasonally adjusted) had gone
below 100,000, which is the lowest since the war and well
below the worst figures for the 1971 and 1976 recessions.
The average fall in job notifications of 11,000 a month in
1980 is all the more disturbing for two reasons. First, there
is no sign yet of any reversal of this underlying trend down-
wards. Second, during previous recessions the number of
vacancies started to rise some months before there was any
fall in the unemployment figures.

The sharpness of the present economic crisis is shown by
the fact that there are already twenty-one registered unemployed for every notified vacancy. This is very much worse
than during the last three peaks of unemployment — 4 to 1
in 1963, 7 to 1 in 1972 and 8.5 to 1 in 1977. While this may
be a fairly consistent indicator of the marked changes over
time, not all the jobs available are reported to the employment service. The official estimate is that there are some
225,000–275,000 jobs available — well over twice as many
as those notified. We do not know to what extent notification
varies with changes in the level of demand, but in the one
detailed survey in 1977 the highest proportion notified was
in the north of England where unemployment was already
high and still rising (*Employment Gazette,* May 1980, p.507).

Even if we accept the official estimate at its highest, there
were still some eight people registered unemployed for every
job available. But this does not mean that the unemployed
had the right skills or lived in the same areas as the jobs that
were to be found (see section 3 of this chapter and section
2.2). There is scarcely any examination of the suitability or
quality of the jobs available — whether for example they are
full-time or part-time, permanent or temporary, demand
'unsocial hours' or provide poor wages and working conditions
(even rates of pay or conditions that are illegal under Wages
Council or Health & Safety legislation). This contrasts with

the frequent claims that many of the unemployed are unsuitable for work or failing to look for it and recurrent official attempts to examine the characteristics of the unemployed, their attitudes and their suitability. Even the latest and most detailed official review (*Employment Gazette,* May 1980, pp.497–508) only mentions the closer examination of the vacancy data largely, it seems, to dismiss this as impracticable. It is important to emphasise that this official neglect is only one example of the general lack of interest among policy analysts as well as policy makers in the job supply side of the labour market.

The Undercount of the Unemployed

The official count of the unemployed also fails to include anyone looking for and available for work if they do not register at their local employment office, however hard they may be searching. The official register also excludes students over the age of 18 only registered for work in their vacations and others not working but considered to have jobs – for example, workers on holiday, or 'temporarily stopped' and on short time working. The government's General Household Survey provides one count of the unregistered unemployed. In 1979 the inclusion of these almost doubled the number of married women out of work, and increased non-married women by one-third and men by one-eighth. Women have less incentive to register because, if they have chosen to pay the reduced National Insurance contribution available to married women, they are not entitled to any insurance benefit. Though this option is now being phased out, many women still continue to pay the reduced rate. The overall effect was to increase total unemployment by one-quarter in 1979.

W. W. Daniel, the Adviser to the House of Lords Select Committee on Unemployment, would put total unemployment even higher (House of Lords Select Committee 1979–1980), vol. ii). Applying his 'best estimate' to the figures for late 1980 would give a total of nearly 2.9 million, probably well over three million by the end of the winter. Daniel also drew attention to those who define themselves as 'inactive' when unemployment is high but declare themselves as looking for work when the job market improves – what the Germans have described as 'the silent reserve'. In one year in the United States five million additional jobs were created but the total unemployed fell by only 1¼ million. Many jobs went to people who had not reported they were unemployed and others began to declare themselves unemployed as the job opportunities emerged (oral evidence to House of Lords Select Committee, 1979–1980, volumes ii and iii).

There is also evidence of a growing 'silent reserve' in the United Kingdom. 'Despite the increase in the population of working age and the slow growth and downturn in employment, there has not been a corresponding increase in unemployment' (*Employment Gazette,* November 1980, p.5). The main reasons for this are thought to be increasing earlier retirement, especially among men, and the withdrawal of married women from the labour force – both likely to be the result of the fall in the demand for workers.

Finally, without the various special temporary employment schemes the numbers out of work would of course be higher still (see section 4.1). At the end of 1979 total unemployment was probably reduced by some 200,000 according to the Department of Employment. There were then about 300,000 people on the different schemes but some would probably not have bothered to register while they were out of work. By the end of October 1980 the number of people covered by these schemes was 256,000 and the Temporary Short Time Working Compensation Scheme was supporting another 412,000 workers.

There has in fact been a massive increase in short-time working to levels well above the previous recession. In mid-September 1980 some 5½ million hours were being lost per week, which was an increase of more than 4 million over the same period in 1979. Even more unusually overtime has also fallen by a third.

All these indicators reflect the serious decline in the economy. The sharp fall in industrial production has been particularly acute in manufacturing, which dropped 11 per cent in 1980 to below its average level for 1968. 'The major contractionary influence in the first half of 1980' has been destocking – the employers reducing production while getting rid of existing stock (*Employment Gazette,* November 1980, p.S2).

The TUC has added the unregistered unemployed to the official register and made estimates of the hours of work lost by short-time etc., and concluded that 3.5 million, not 2 million is the 'real' total. *The Times* has also suggested a total over 3 million (26 November 1980). By contrast the Institute of Economic Affairs has stated that 'two million is one million'. The main groups they remove, who are 'on the register for a large number of reasons, not closely associated with unemployment at all', are nearly 300,000 school leavers; 230,000 who have been out of work less than four weeks, described as 'not strictly "unemployed" but changing jobs'; occupational pensioners and some '125,000 unemployables and 100,000 who would be reluctant to work unless they can get a "good" job' (Miller, 1980).

Claims of official overcount have tended to emerge when unemployment is rising (for a critique of earlier claims, see Deacon, 1980b, and Showler, 1980). The issues raised are considered in later chapters which discuss the different groups and their experience of it. I have used the official figures here and throughout the book, except where clearly indicated, because – whatever their shortcomings – they have been collected regularly and with relatively little change since 1948. They therefore provide the best available guide to trends and changes over the last generation.

Comparison with other countries provides a valuable perspective on unemployment in Britain and, incidentally, requires that we take the broader, not the narrower, view of the official statistics in order to bring them more into line with the definition recommended by the International Labour Office. Over the past twenty years there has been a tendency for unemployment to converge, at least among the nine countries studied by Sorrentino (1980). But even the latest figures adjusted for comparison show a considerable variation from 2 per cent to over 9 per cent (see Table 1). Britain, France and Australia have moved into the group of countries with higher unemployment over the last decade, with Britain moving above all the other eight countries in November 1980. The difference in the changes over time strongly suggests

TABLE 1: UNEMPLOYMENT RATES ADJUSTED TO US CONCEPTS, 1960–80

Year	Great Britain	United States	Canada	Australia	Japan	France	Germany	Italy	Sweden
1960	2.2%	5.5	7.0	1.6	1.7	1.8	1.1	3.8	NA
1961	2.0	6.7	7.1	3.0	1.5	1.6	.6	3.2	1.4
1962	2.8	6.5	5.9	2.4	1.3	1.5	.6	2.8	1.5
1963	3.4	5.7	5.5	2.3	1.3	1.3	.5	2.4	1.7
1964	2.5	5.2	4.7	1.4	1.2	1.5	.4	2.6	1.5
1965	2.2	4.5	3.9	1.3	1.2	1.6	.3	3.5	1.2
1966	2.3	3.8	3.4	1.5	1.4	1.9	.3	3.8	1.6
1967	3.4	3.8	3.8	1.6	1.3	2.0	1.3	3.4	2.1
1968	3.3	3.6	4.5	1.5	1.2	2.6	1.4	3.4	2.2
1969	3.0	3.5	4.4	1.5	1.1	2.4	.9	3.3	1.9
1970	3.1	4.9	5.7	1.6	1.2	2.6	.8	3.1	1.5
1971	3.7	5.9	6.2	1.8	1.3	2.8	.8	3.1	2.6
1972	4.1	5.6	6.2	2.6	1.4	2.9	.8	3.6	2.7
1973	2.9	4.9	5.6	2.3	1.3	2.8	.8	3.4	2.5
1974	2.9	5.6	5.4	2.7	1.4	3.0	1.7	2.8	2.0
1975	4.1	8.5	6.9	4.9	1.9	4.3	3.6	3.2	1.6
1976	5.5	7.7	7.1	4.8	2.0	4.7	3.6	3.6	1.6
1977	6.2*	7.0	8.1	5.6	2.0	5.0	3.8*	3.4	1.8
1978	6.1*	6.0	8.4	6.3	2.3	5.4	3.7*	3.7	2.2
1979	5.8*	5.8	7.5	6.2	2.1	6.2*	3.3*	4.3	2.1
1980 Jan.	6.1	6.1	7.4	NA	1.9	6.3	3.1	6.0	1.8
April	6.8	7.5	7.7	NA	2.0	6.6	3.2	5.9	2.0
July	7.7	7.6	7.6	NA	2.1	6.6	3.4	6.0	1.9
Nov.	9.3	7.5	7.3	NA	2.2 (Oct.)	6.5 (Oct.)	3.7	NA	2.4

Notes: * Annual figures preliminary. NA – not available.
Monthly figures for France, Germany and Great Britain are calculated by applying annual adjustment factors to current published data and therefore should be viewed as less precise indicators of unemployment under U.S. concepts than the annual figures.
Source: Sorrentino (1980, p.170, updated December 1980). For an account of the adjustments, see Sorrentino (1980) pp.168–9 and 209–12.

that the increased unemployment in Britain cannot simply be a result of the international recession.

Unemployment Forecasts

'Jobs going at rate of 3,000 a day' and 'two jobs lost every minute' were the *Guardian* and the *Times* headlines to the announcement of the November 1980 unemployment figures. Forecasters who are brave enough to discern any light at the end of the tunnel are becoming harder to find. Fewer forecasters are prepared to offer a prediction for 1981, although all of these expect a continuing increase. In fact the majority forecast is one-third higher than that made for 1980 (based on data supplied from Cooper, forthcoming). Even those who see the beginning of a recovery of business confidence and a sustained reduction in the level of inflation emphasise that these improvements may have very little effect on the totals of unemployed. So the prospects for the unemployed and many other workers are all the more gloomy as the main issue for argument among forecasters is not whether unemployment will increase, but how quickly and by how much.

Predictions of an industrial Armageddon with dramatically higher unemployment by the end of this century are receiving very much more attention than the pessimistic forecasts of the past, and not simply because of the recent sharp rise in unemployment and the growing evidence of a recession declining into a slump. Equally disturbingly, those who were dismissed as 'prophets of doom' in the last five years can point to their generally greater accuracy in predicting the present levels of unemployment. The Cambridge Economic Policy Group appears to have displayed an accuracy in forecasting that has disconcerted many more traditional economists who continue to attack the Group's policy proposals while having to admit their own poorer record in forecasting. In their 1980 Review the Group stated that the maintenance of existing economic policies would bring unemployment to 3½ million by 1985. In December 1980, their Director, Wynne Godley, stated that 'if unemployment goes on rising at the average rate of the last quarter (i.e. at 'only' 110,000 a month) the headline total will read 3.2 million in July next year' (*Guardian,* 1 December 1980). By contrast, the Treasury and those who often seem to appear as its spokesmen – the Chancellor of the Exchequer and the Chief Secretary to the Treasury – have tended to underestimate the seriousness of the problem to a remarkable extent. Little more than three years ago the Treasury was still keeping to its official prediction of a decline in unemployment to around 3 per cent, or 700,000, by the end of the 1970s. Even after the last Budget the Treasury failed to anticipate the acceleration in rising unemployment, despite the wealth of evidence offered it on this point. At present, the Treasury is said to expect unemployment to rise to around 2.75 million by the end of 1981, although the latest independent forecasts would support higher predictions. Not one of the twenty-one forecasts made in autumn 1979 expected a drop in unemployment during 1980, although only the very highest proved accurate (Cooper, 1980, p.17).

The prospect continues to look very poor for what is called the medium term. The Warwick Group offered a range between 2.6 and 3 million unemployed for 1985 in analyses prepared before the 1980 Budget (Lindley, 1980, p.32). Their own arguments for these calculations in the light of subsequent economic policies and developments would tend to support their more gloomy forecasts. In their latest Review, the National Institute of Economic and Social Research state that unemployment could climb to more than 3.5 million by the end of 1985 'if government policies are not changed and world trade remains sluggish' (*Guardian,* 28 November 1980). By the end of 1980 the very cautious Manpower Services Commission was taking a very depressed view and their Chief Executive of Training Services expected unemployment to remain at 'historically high levels' throughout the 1980s leading to 'wasted human potential on an unprecedented scale' (*Guardian,* 24 November 1980).

Comparison with the predictions for other countries is, if anything, even less encouraging. Forecasters generally predict a greater increase in unemployment for the United Kingdom than most industrial market economies, and these predictions come from international as well as national groups. Of fourteen countries only Spain is expected to have a very much higher increase than the United Kingdom. Switzerland is slightly higher with a 20 per cent increase, but this only means a rise from 0.5 per cent to 0.6 per cent! Belgium, the United States and the UK are expected to increase their unemployment between 1980 and 1981 by just under 20 per cent with both the UK and the USA showing little, if any, growth in gross domestic product (Cooper, forthcoming).

The inaccuracy of past predictions must obviously be kept in mind, although predictions of gloom and slump can of course become self-fulfilling prophecies by depressing already diminishing business confidence. But it should be emphasised that the models from which the forecasts are derived can only build on present trends. They can, for example, take account of the increasing number of school leavers expected to enter the labour force in the next couple of years and any other available evidence of this type. They are, however, 'surprisefree'. Any forecast made before the Iranian revolution, for instance, made no allowance for the impact of this on the supply of oil and the doubling in energy prices that placed yet further pressure on the economy and deepened the recession. Projection of existing trends also assume the maintenance of existing government policies, and these can obviously be changed. Indeed, there are some grounds for thinking that the accuracy of the more gloomy forecasts in the second half of the 1970s was due in part to the changes in government policy that led to increases in unemployment and in part to the international developments, particularly connected with the price of oil, that only worsened the crisis.

The reason for emphasising these points is the danger that an increasing number of those who hold power in private and public industry and in government, and significant groups abroad, come to act as if these forecasts were inexorable developments. In addition, many of those now challenging us to 'think the unthinkable' and plan for a society with 4 or 5 million unemployed have generally tended to accept these forecasts as inevitable, and as being a further reason for abandoning the goal of full employment.

1.2   THE UNEQUAL BURDEN OF UNEMPLOYMENT

To understand what being out of work means and how it affects the lives of the unemployed and their families, we need first of all to know who make up the total out of work. With unemployment rising so fast, there has been increasing attention to the 'new' unemployed. Skilled and technical workers in companies that have never experienced redundancy are now having to join the dole queue. 'Recession is no longer a respecter of power and position' and there is a 'growing army of redundant executives. In previous recessions the executive . . . has usually remained above the blood-letting on the factory floor' (*Sunday Times,* 14 December 1980). The experience of redundancy and then unemployment for these people is often harsh and bitter but the extension of any problem to a group that has previously been protected from it is generally likely to receive closer attention than the experience of those whose vulnerability might be described as endemic, given the structure and workings of our society. It is important therefore to examine who generally make up the unemployed before focusing on particular groups.

The first and most crucial point for understanding the direct impact of unemployment is its unequal distribution across society. Some eighteen months ago, when unemployment was less than two-thirds of the present figure, it was estimated what a sharing of that level of unemployment would have meant. Everyone could have expected to be out of work once every six years, or eight spells a lifetime. In fact, at that time just 3 per cent of the labour force were bearing 70 per cent of the total weeks of unemployment a year (Metcalf, 1980, p.24).

It is important to emphasise that those most likely to be unemployed are people in low-paying and insecure jobs, the very young and the oldest in the labour force, people from ethnic or racial minorities, people from among the disabled and handicapped, and generally those with the least skills and living in the most depressed areas. Unemployment strikes, and strikes most harshly and frequently, those who are among the poorest and least powerful in the labour force and in society as a whole. Worse still, the experience of being out of work may trap people at the bottom of society as if in some underclass, and most will go back into jobs as poorly or even more poorly paid.

This very unequal burden of unemployment needs all the closer attention because of the frequency with which it is completely overlooked. Twice in two minutes unemployment was described as 'the price we have to pay' for past failings by the Deputy Chairman of the Stock Exchange during a radio interview at the announcement of the monthly unemployment figures on 25 November, 1980, and I have noted many similar comments recently. 'Economists and public policy makers debate the question: how much unemployment can the country stand? Strictly speaking, it is not "the country" that is being asked to "stand unemployment". Unemployment does not, like air pollution or God's gentle rain, fall uniformly upon everyone . . . it strikes from underneath, and its strikes particularly at those at the bottom of our society' (Liebow, 1970, p.28).

The disproportionate concentration among the lower paid has often been discounted when unemployment is rising. While these workers may have borne the brunt of previously low levels of unemployment, it is pointed out that higher unemployment has hit many more better-paid workers. This of course is perfectly true. The sharp increase in major redundancies means that many highly skilled and non-manual workers from larger firms that pay higher wages have been thrown out of work. But many more low-paid have also continued to join the ranks of the unemployed. Over the last twenty years the risk of being unemployed has been very much greater for the unskilled, and they have often formed more than half the total unemployed. Even at the present very high level, their share has not fallen below two-fifths, and is generally much higher in regions with the highest unemployment. This proportion is probably still at least three times their share of the overall labour force.

The much heavier concentration of unemployment among the low-paid has continued to emerge as unemployment has risen first above half a million, next above 1 million, and then above 1½ million. In March 1979, with unemployment nationally just under 6 per cent, or 1½ million, a study in eighteen urban areas concluded 'what is most striking is that the intimate relationship between poverty and unemployment demonstrated at a time of low unemployment in 1973 still persists when the rate of unemployment has risen to a much higher level' (Smith, 1980, p.20).

Another argument has also tended to discount the unequal burden of unemployment. Most research only tells us about the *stock* of unemployed – the people out of work at the time of a survey. Some will have been unemployed a few weeks, others a few months or even years. But the stock may look very different from the *flow* – the people becoming unemployed on one particular day. Many of these will only be out of work a few days and are less likely to appear in studies of the unemployed. These people, it is suggested, are also less likely to be concentrated among those with below-average earnings. Again there is a considerable element of truth in this point. Men with more skills are likely to have higher pay and to find work more quickly. In March 1979, unskilled manual workers were roughly six times as likely to become unemployed for a lengthy period as non-manual workers, who were generally more highly paid; and within each occupational level those with badly paid jobs were less likely to escape unemployment as quickly (Smith, 1980).

Nevertheless, the one national analysis we have of the flow of unemployed shows very clearly that workers with below-average earnings are much more likely to become unemployed than the better paid. The Department of Health and Social Security carried out a most detailed study of a national sample of men registering as unemployed in the late autumn of 1978 (referred to below as the Cohort Study – see Moylan and Davies, 1980, 1981). The male unemployment rate at that time was almost 7 per cent, well above the average for the 1970s, let alone the two previous decades. Yet as many as one-half of the unemployed men reporting past earnings had had wages so low that they fell into the bottom fifth of the national earnings distribution; 1 in 3 had had wages below £50 a week, compared with only 1 in 10 of the male working population. Very few had had earnings in the top fifth of male earnings. Many without earnings in the previous year had not worked because of sickness. In general, earnings of the unemployed were well below the national average for every age group, and so their low pay is not explained by the much higher unemployment rates among young people. They also tended to have lower earnings than the average for their occupation, as other surveys have found.

Four to five months after the men had first registered, half were still out of work, but a third had found a full-time job. Although there were considerable changes of occupation in industry, there was little improvement in pay. Nearly half returned to earnings at the same level, but in real terms, allowing for inflation, at least one-third had taken jobs that meant a cut in their earnings. This was generally more likely among those who had been low earners in the past (Moylan and Davies, 1981).

We do not have such detailed evidence for women, but there is no reason to expect much difference in the pattern. Besides, given their much lower average earnings, the proportion of unemployed women with past earnings at or above the average for men seems bound to be very much smaller.

The significance of these low earnings becomes all the greater when account is taken of the extent of repeated unemployment. For very many people, being unemployed is not a rare occurrence in a generally secure working career. The most recent evidence comes from the DHSS Cohort Study (Moylan and Davies, 1980). Over half the men becoming unemployed in 1978 had been out of work before within the previous twelve months and more than three-quarters had been out of work at least once in the previous five years. Over two-fifths had been unemployed at least twice before and one-quarter at least three times. In addition, nearly 1 in 8 men had been off work sick within the previous twelve months.

This evidence is particularly valuable in helping us to understand the impact of unemployment in Britain today, because it warns us against dismissing the short-term unemployed as the 'frictional' unemployed, simply experiencing a brief period out of work between jobs. In consequence, some analysts remove all those out of work for under four weeks from the official total on the grounds that they could be suffering no hardship (e.g. Miller, 1980). Taking account of the findings on repeated unemployment from official and independent research, requires a very different assessment of the issues. If most unemployed have not been in well-paid jobs and many have been out of work during the recent past, they are not very likely to be well protected against their present unemployment, however brief it is. Almost half the men who became unemployed in autumn 1978 said they had no savings at all. And when out of work, they do not receive the highest benefits because these are related to past annual earnings (see section 4.2). Since redundancy payments are also linked to previous earnings and length of continuous service, with a minimum requirement of two years, it is not surprising that less than 5 per cent received any payment at all (Moylan and Davies, 1980; see also Daniel, 1974).

Particular attention has been given to these two issues of earnings and previous unemployment because the evidence on the concentration of unemployment runs strongly counter to general impressions. We have to recognise that those who remain out of work for many months may be all the more vulnerable to poverty and deprivation because they have very few resources. Those out of work only a few weeks or a couple of months may still experience hardship because they had low pay in their last job, and even that may have been interrupted by loss of earnings due to sickness or unemployment. The role of income maintenance programmes during such interruptions to earnings thus becomes all the more important, and the effect of these will be examined in section 4.2.

The argument that this is just part of the 'natural' order of things has to explain why the concentration of unemployment among the lower paid should be higher in the UK than in some other countries. Careful comparison with evidence for the United States and Canada shows that, although the risk of unemployment is still greater the lower the worker comes in the earnings hierarchy, it is by no means as unequally distributed in these two countries as in the United Kingdom (Smee, 1980). At the same national level of unemployment, the average worker has a much greater likelihood of being out of work in the United States than here. The average duration of unemployment is less than in Britain, so that more workers are out of work but for a shorter period of time. This should lead us to look even more carefully at the effects of this concentration, and the extent to which it is compensated for. One political consequence seems to be that the greater immunity to unemployment of the better-off may help to account for the relatively low level of concern about unemployment, despite the dramatic increases over the last seven years. As a result, there may be less recognition in Britain of the full social and economic costs of unemployment.

1.3   THE GEOGRAPHY OF UNEMPLOYMENT

Over the last thirty years the level of unemployment throughout the United Kingdom has changed dramatically, but there has been remarkably little change in the geographical incidence of unemployment. Those areas that tended to bear the heaviest unemployment in the 1950s and 1960s are still hardest hit in the 1980s. Since the war, Northern Ireland has consistently had by far the highest level of unemployment. For many years it was three or four times the national average; only recently has it fallen to below twice the average (Trewsdale, 1980). Practically every year for the last thirty, the North, Wales, Scotland and the North West have suffered the highest rates within Britain. In recent years the unemployment level in the West Midlands, with a dependence on manufacturing that kept it particularly prosperous in the early post-war years, has deteriorated sharply — from 1.8 per cent in 1973, to 5.6 per cent in 1979 to 9.4 per cent in November 1980. During the 1950s, Wales appeared to be escaping more quickly than some of the other areas most hard hit by the 1930s, but the Welsh valleys and areas like Port Talbot have suffered particularly severely over the last decade. The benefits of the oil industry have made some impact in Scotland but not enough to lift it from its position of one of the regions with the highest unemployment.

It has been the persistent regional imbalance in unemployment since the war that has made the claims and complaints of 'full' or 'overfull' employment so mistaken. Discussion tends to focus on the short-term changes in the rankings

Figure 2: Unemployment by region, November 1980 and 1979.

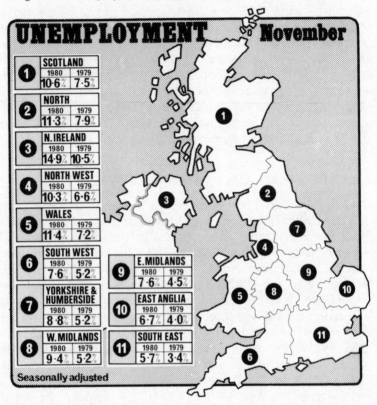

Source: *Financial Times*, 26 November 1980

rather than on the long-term impact. This can be particularly misleading because public attention is usually focused more closely on unemployment while it is rising, when differences between regions tend to diminish. This is brought out very clearly in Figure 2. Northern Ireland had almost 15 per cent unemployment in November 1980. But the rate at which unemployment grew over the previous twelve months was only 42 per cent, the slowest but one of all the regions. The North West and the West Midlands experienced a much faster rise, although their overall level was still not two-thirds of the level in Ulster. Unemployment in the South East and East

TABLE 2: MALE UNEMPLOYMENT RATES BY DURATION
FOR EACH REGION, OCTOBER 1980

	Per cent of male employees unemployed		
	All	*Long-term — 6 months or more*	*Very long-term 1 year or more*
	%	%	%
Northern Ireland	18.4	8.5	5.5
Wales	13.3	5.0	2.9
North	13.2	5.9	3.7
Scotland	12.3	5.2	3.1
North West	12.3	5.2	3.1
West Midlands	10.7	4.0	2.2
Yorkshire and Humberside	10.3	3.8	2.2
South West	8.9	3.2	2.0
East Midlands	8.9	3.3	1.9
East Anglia	7.8	2.5	1.4
South East	6.8	2.1	1.1
United Kingdom	9.9	3.8	2.2
Numbers	1,414,191	539,736	313,591

Source: *Employment Gazette,* November 1980

Anglia now averages about 6 per cent compared with 1.2 per cent over the twenty years to 1968. This is a fivefold increase over the years of low unemployment, but even during those years annual unemployment in Northern Ireland never fell as low as unemployment in the South East in November 1980. The difference between the regions which have long had higher unemployment and those with lower rates is even greater when one considers the proportions of workers unemployed for six months and one year (see Table 2).

The impact of unemployment on families is even more severe in regions with the higher rates. Long-term and very long-term unemployment among men aged 25—54, who are most likely to be married with dependent children, is further above the average for all men in the most depressed areas. In Northern Ireland 55 per cent of these men have been out of work for at least six months.

There may of course be considerable variations within regions. Even in the South East when unemployment stood at 5.6 per cent in September 1980, Chatham, Ramsgate and Southend had over 9 per cent while Hertford, St. Albans, Watford, Slough and Crawley had under 4 per cent. Within London there is great variation between depressed inner-city areas and some of the more affluent suburbs. This reflects not only the higher proportion of unskilled and semi-skilled living towards the centre but the general move of employment opportunities to the outer ring. In regions of much higher unemployment, the inner cities may be even worse affected. The average 10 per cent unemployment in the North West for September 1980 included 15 per cent in Liverpool as a whole and claims of over 50 or 60 per cent in some parts of the centre of the city. Within Scotland, unemployment is generally much higher on the West coast, with parts of Strathclyde amongst the worst hit in the whole of the United Kingdom. The Grampian region, however, claims to be the main, if not the only, growth area in the country at present. In mid-November 1980 the regional planners predicted some 16,500 new jobs during this decade and spoke of 'a period of unparalleled economic vitality' in an area that bore more than its fair share of the inter-war depression. Even here though, there are doubts that the 'oil-fired economy' will be enough to protect the region against the recession. In the same week as the optimistic forecasts were announced, 'the first traditional industrial casualty' appeared when it was announced that 320 jobs would be lost with the closure of a paper mill in Aberdeen in February 1981. Some employers have claimed that the boost to the local economy by the oil industry will only help to kill off some of the older-established companies because Grampian has lost its development area status (*Guardian,* 17 November 1980).

Despite the variations within regions however, the basic pattern remains in the comparison of local areas across regions. The Department of Employment publishes unemployment rates for 182 separate areas in the United Kingdom. In September 1980 only eight of these were below half the national unemployment level and all but one were in the South East. There were twelve areas with levels twice the national average and eight of these were in Northern Ireland. Only 1 in every 11 local areas reported for the South East,

East Anglia and the South West had levels above the national average in September 1980. This compares with 9 out of every 10 areas in the rest of the United Kingdom, apart from the East and West Midlands.

Living With High Unemployment

What it means to live in an area of persistently high unemployment was brought home to me in my first interviews with men out of work in Britain in late 1963 (North Tyneside CDP, 1978). North Shields on Tyneside had been chosen for the survey because the North East of England had been badly hit by the sharp rise in unemployment during the winter of 1962/3. Towns with very high unemployment had been deliberately avoided; on the measures available, North Shields seemed typical of the region as a whole but had *less* long-term unemployment. I prepared my questions to find out how workers and their families were coping with the crisis of a sudden increase in unemployment.

My mistake became evident very quickly. Very few of the ninety-two unemployed men I spoke to had not been out of work before. More than one-quarter of the previous five years had been totally unproductive for this sample of unemployed men – an average of 1 year and 5 months had been spent 'signing on at the dole'. The information given by the men was confirmed by data from the employment exchange records.

As total unemployment has increased, its incidence over time may well have grown even faster. In 1975/6 a second sample of unemployed was drawn in the same way in the same area (North Tyneside CDP, 1978). North Shields had been hit much more severely by the deterioration in the economy in the intervening twelve years and unemployment had risen well above the regional rate to 15 per cent. We were only able to identify spells of unemployment over the previous three and not five years because of changes in the employment service. But more than 1 in 3 of the second sample had been mainly or wholly out of work for the three years. In 1963/4 this group had formed less than 1 in 10 of those interviewed.

In the second study we also interviewed men in work and made an estimate of the extent of unemployment throughout the southern half of North Shields over the previous three years. Barely half of the men of labour-force age were likely to have escaped any unemployment, while 1 in 8 were likely to have been frequently, mainly or continuously out of work.

The original sample had also suffered badly amid the higher unemployment. We were able to follow up the experience in and out of work of at least two-thirds of the men till their re-interview, or their retirement or death. Only fifteen of the sixty-eight men had been successful in avoiding a significant amount of time out of work. Eighteen of them had been unemployed for all or most of the twelve years since their first interview. For the majority of men there was work but no security: 'going through spells of unemployment was the norm' (North Tyneside CDP, 1978, p.221, and Sinfield, 1970). Those who were most vulnerable in the past seemed least likely to have escaped unemployment and were much more liable to yet further unemployment. The picture that emerges is a depressing one of a downward spiral. It illustrates well what may happen in a community with above-average unemployment for many years, and how further increases in unemployment will generally hit these groups yet again. When North Shields was originally chosen, its unemployment rate was close to that for the whole of the Northern region, and the level of long-term unemployment was no higher than the average for Britain.

1.4   LET THEM MOVE TO WORK?

One of the most persistent criticisms of the unemployed is that they will not move to find work. Fresh currency was given to this charge by the Prime Minister in a fighting speech to the Welsh Conservative Party at Swansea in July (*Sunday Times,* 20 July 1980). Of course in the past we have exported our unemployment to what were then labour-hungry colonies, and some cities virtually deported their able-bodied paupers. Many different schemes based at home or abroad helped to attract unemployed, especially to the countries of the old Commonwealth. During the inter-war recession, for example,

Dr Barnado's moved many boys to Australia or Canada. Even within Britain there was encouragement for farm colonies and the establishment of various forms of co-operatives in rural areas.

Despite the widespread mythology of the immobile worker, very many have moved. Analyses of the 1971 census show that about one in eight people had moved home in the last year — a rate quite comparable to most other industrial economies. There is also evidence that 'migration is related to the economic climate of the region' (Lindley, ed., 1980, p.168). For the last generation the population of Scotland has tended to decline mainly because of emigration to the South or overseas. The north-east of England has also long been an exporter of labour, and rising unemployment still brings an increase in emigration. In 1980 six hundred people a month were 'leaving the country from the North East — mostly to seek jobs in Canada or Australia'. The evidence from Consulate offices shows that the rate of emigration doubled in 1980. Most of the emigrants are professional or skilled workers, aged between 25 and 35. 'These are the very people the area and the country will need if ever the economy turns and the country tries to get back on its feet' concludes Gordon Adam, the Northumberland MEP, who carried out the survey (*Labour Weekly,* 28 November 1980).

The New Towns provide particularly strong evidence of mobility. Indeed the success of the New Towns around London in attracting labour from the more depressed areas in the 1950s and early 1960s may well have done much more to intensify the structural unemployment problems of those areas than any immobility on the part of workers. By and large it was the more skilled, physically able and younger workers who moved, leaving a very unbalanced age structure. But these moves are not always clear successes. Corby in Northamptonshire quickly became a thriving steel town known as 'Little Scotland' because of its success in attracting workers from the North. In October 1980 almost one in five of the Corby labour force was out of work — this was the highest rate recorded in any of the 169 separate local areas (excluding Northern Ireland) for which the Department of Employment regularly publishes statistics. Although the collapse of the Corby labour market may be particularly notorious, there are going to be many more areas which were designated for growth only a few years ago where workers who have moved for jobs and housing will find themselves both out of work and unable to sell their homes because there are no jobs to attract the house buyers. Fort William provides one recent example.

But, however willing workers or unemployed may be to move, structural and other changes in British society and in the economy are making it increasingly difficult for them. In the past the availability of privately rented housing made labour mobility much easier but this sector of housing has declined dramatically this century. Privately rented accommodation for families especially has virtually disappeared. The steady growth in owner occupation since the war has been accompanied by very high differentials in the price of private housing, between, very roughly, those areas with jobs and those without. For most would-be movers, therefore, the major problem is that, with the sum they can raise from selling their own property in a declining area, they cannot buy any housing in the areas that have jobs. At the least it would mean a massive increase in their mortgage payments – if they were fortunate enough to get one. This is illustrated by comparing the cheaper housing advertised in North Shields on Tyneside, where unemployment is over 10 per cent, with Watford in South-west Herts, which has less than half this level.

TABLE 3: CHEAPEST FAMILY HOMES IN WATFORD AND
NORTH SHIELDS NEWSPAPERS, DECEMBER 1980

Watford Observer 5/12/80	*Shields Weekly News 4/12/80*
£18,000. – Centrally situated 3-bedroomed terrace house, in need of modernisation and refurbishment.	**WALLSEND, NORTHUMBERLAND AVENUE.** A compact mid terraced house in quiet pedestrian street, in need of a little attention, comprising: Entrance hall, lounge with gas fire, dining room, kitchen, two bedrooms, bathroom/w.c. Small front garden, rear yard. Price . . . . **£8,900 o.n.o.**

Watford Observer 5/12/80   *Shields Weekly News 4/12/80*

£19,500. — Spacious second-floor flat; central heating and double glazing, good decorative order, near station and town centre.

£22,000. — Delightful terrace cottage with 3 bedrooms, in very nice order and ideal for the first-time purchaser.

£22,500. — Terrace house in good order; rewired, new windows, centrally situated.

£23,000. — Realistically priced 3-bedroomed semi-detached with integral garage. Rewired and new roof. Large cellar.

£24,750. — Superb 3-bedroomed end terrace house in a quiet cul-de-sac with possible space for garage. Rewired, replumbed, new windows, etc. 70ft. rear garden.

DENE CRESCENT, WALLSEND. Vacant possession of upper flat with central heating. Three rooms, kitchen. Combined bathroom with w.c. Lower flat well let. Car standing. Price **£13,500**

NEWCASTLE STREET. Modernised terraced house with lounge, dining room, kitchen and central heating. First floor: Three bedrooms, bathroom and w.c., attic bedroom. Price **£13,500**

NORTH SHIELDS, ALMA PLACE. Spacious three bedroom terrace house convenient for town centre. Entrance lobby and hall, 3 reception rooms with gas fires, kitchen, bathroom and sep. w.c. Garden and onsite parking. All carpets and curtains. **£13,500**

WHITBY STREET. Attractive corner terraced house. Recently converted and modernised, in good decorative order. Two reception, three bedrooms, fitted kitchen, new bathroom. Price **£14,000**

NORTH SHIELDS, FRANK PLACE. Well modernised spacious four-bedroom terrace house convenient for town centre. Entrance lobby and hall, three reception rooms (one with gas fire), 14ft. kitchen, one bedroom with built-in wardrobe, bathroom with primrose suite and separate shower compartment. Gardens. Garage and onsite parking. All carpets. **£15,500**

Watford Observer 5/12/80	*Shields Weekly News 4/12/80*
£24,950. – Superb end terrace property with above average accommodation; 3 reception-rooms, 3 bedrooms. Possible hard standing for car.	**FERN AVENUE.** Modernised, well decorated semi with front and rear gardens, modern windows, rewired and gas central heating, lounge with bay window and feature fireplace, breakfast room/kitchen with modern built-in cupboards. First floor: Three bedrooms, bathroom and w.c. with coloured suite . . . **£18,900**

For most unemployed and manual workers who might be considering a move, council housing is really the only option given the marked decline in the privately rented sector. But it is here that the greatest problems arise with many local authorities still operating a form of the Poor Law Settlement Act. In other words, nobody can qualify to go on the council housing waiting list until they have spent some time in that local authority. All the inducements and cajolery of central government over the years have largely failed, and the government is now having to introduce legislation to tackle this problem. There are an amazing variety of procedures used by local authorities in determining priority for the available council housing but few give any or much credit to 'key' or incoming workers.

Very many authorities use a groups-plus-points scheme where priority is awarded within different groups, such as homeless, substandard accommodation, medical need, over-crowding or essential workers. In Scotland three-quarters of the housing authorities use some form of grouping but less than a third of these include key or incoming workers as a group.

The date order scheme simply ranks applications in the order that they are received. Most local authorities no longer operate with the simple version of this scheme but combine it with the others. Key workers may often be accepted on the housing list but then find the long waiting period creates considerable problems for them and their families. They may be forced into very expensive or alternatively very sub-standard temporary accommodation with their families during this waiting period or else separated from them by long distances. Both may create considerable family problems as well as financial hardship, and key workers have often returned home as soon as they have been able to obtain a job just because they cannot find adequate accommodation.

It is not surprising that the effect of council housing on labour mobility has been attacked. In Scotland, for example, 'a primary cause' of higher structural unemployment 'is connected with the very high proportion of the Scottish labour force who live in council houses'. 'The Scottish obsession with cheap public sector housing may come a close second to the Berlin Wall as the most formidable obstacle to geographical mobility yet devised by man'. These quotations appear in a report of the Scottish Economic Planning Department in October 1979 which itself cautiously concludes that 'the local authority sector did have a significant constraining effect on the mobility of labour in Scotland . . . this resulted from characteristics inherent in tenure itself rather than the personal and social characteristics of its households' (Robertson, 1979, pp.3 and 36). The Scottish Special Housing Association appears to have been able to make relatively little contribution to solving this problem. These difficulties are made all the greater by developments in recent years which have very much restricted the growth of council housing and hampered its adequate maintenance. These can only exacerbate the problem because there are many other urgent and pressing demands on local authorities from other people in housing need. While the Prime Minister therefore attacks the unemployed for their failure to move, the policies of her own government are already making worse the very difficulties that inhibit mobility. The encouragement to buy council housing may also increase the number of people with mortgage commitments who are unable to move out of declining areas.

Someone who interviews those out of work is probably less likely to find the ones who successfully got away to another job. I have been struck, however, by the number of men who have worked outside their home area and have moved briefly or attempted to move. Clearly it is easier at some stages of one's life than others. Younger men talk about the need to decide whether to move or to stay and settle down with a family. The discouragement to mobility is all the greater for those who depend upon personal contacts to find work (see section 2.2). Generally the unskilled find many fewer jobs outside the area notified through local job centres.

This, as well as the housing problem, may explain why so many of the workers I met who moved to find jobs stayed with relatives who had made a previous move, increasing their chances of finding work through them (see section 2.2). The cuts in social services, particularly in relation to the increasing needs of the growing number of elderly, are also likely to act as a restraint on the traditional patterns of mobility. They force the younger members to choose between abandoning elderly relatives at a time when the government is calling on families to take on even more of the community care role and moving to a new job when there can be no guarantee of security. This raises the whole question of the personal and social costs of moving. It is part of the social distance with which we tend to view the majority of the unemployed that we overlook these issues. The only exception is the discussion of executive mobility and the need for special counselling for redundant executives. Here the personal problems of having to move receive more detailed and sympathetic attention – the question of the spouse's career, the education of the children, the problems and costs of the move, etc. (*Management Today,* June 1980: The High Price of Mobility).

CHAPTER TWO

Being Out of Work

2.1 THE EXPERIENCE OF UNEMPLOYMENT

Of all the reactions to being out of work for the first time, surprise is the most common. This point has emerged in every study of unemployment, certainly since the war, that I have ever read. It indicates the lack of awareness about the problems of being out of work among the rest of the population and may help to account for the generally unsympathetic and often very suspicious attitude towards the unemployed. As one apprenticed tradesman in his early twenties commented in 1979: 'It's changed my attitudes to the unemployed. I used to think they were just skivers and was quite a lot against them, but now that I've experienced it, it's no joke, man' (Newcastle, 1980, p.35). Another in North Tyneside said, 'once you've been on the dole yourself, you begin to think differently about the other people there. You can't help it, and you realise that perhaps they can't either'. It was the actual experience of unemployment that led these workers to alter their own opinions of what it was like to be out of work and so to start breaking down their own stereotypes of the unemployed.

Some men spoke with considerable contempt of the others they met at the dole but this distancing did not seem to appear among those who had been out of work for a couple of months or more. It is perhaps more common among those who seem to feel the acutest shame and stigma at being out of work themselves. 'This feeling that people are looking down on you was sometimes accompanied by the ironic comment that the respondent himself had probably done the same when he was working' (Newcastle, 1980, p.32). Keen awareness of the status of being unemployed comes through in interview after interview. Men who have lost their jobs, and are officially registered as unemployed while looking for work, have gone out of their way to emphasise that they are not unemployed but redundant.

Each time unemployment tends to rise, there are suggestions that the stigma of unemployment has been substantially reduced, which not only eases the strain and tension for the unemployed but reduces the social pressure on them to get back to work at the first possible opportunity. To some observers, increased unemployment itself is seen as acting to reduce the speed with which the total declines.

It is therefore important to emphasise the continuing feelings of stigma and shame expressed by many of the unemployed. These feelings may be reduced at a major redundancy but the quotations above show that it may return very quickly. Joe Kenyon has been giving welfare rights advice for many years and is continuing to get letters or phone calls that begin 'I have never been out of work' or 'my husband has never been out of work'. 'A harmless thing to say, you might think. But think about it some more. "Never been out of work" – does it mean that this should carry some kind of privilege, as against the one who has been out of work before?' If one can claim, with an injured pride, that this is the first experience of unemployment, then one is establishing more deserving status. The implication is that those with repeated experiences of unemployment have a more questionable claim for sympathy and special help.

Obviously, the impact of unemployment on those out of work and their families varies enormously. There is a great difference between two weeks and two years on the dole. It will be all the greater if the short-term unemployed has already found work before his last job ended while the long-term unemployed has become disabled or finds his skill is no longer needed, and may despair of ever working again. There will also be differences between individuals because of their different personalities. But one general thesis has begun to appear more and more frequently in discussions of the unemployed and is now in danger of becoming part of the conventional but unproven wisdom about the impact of unemployment on the individual. In the late 1930s a hypothesis on the 'psychology of unemployment' emerged from a detailed review of literature by Eisenberg and Lazersfeld:

> First there is shock, which is followed by an active hunt for a job, during which the individual is still optimistic and unresigned; he still maintains an unbroken attitude. Second, when all efforts fail, the individual becomes pessimistic, anxious and suffers active distress; this is the most crucial state of all. And, third, the individual becomes fatalistic and adapts himself to his new state with a narrower scope. He now has a broken attitude. [1938, p.378]

Despite their cautious qualifications to this hypothesis, stressing the very poor quality and imprecision of much of the research, and despite the fact that others, such as E. Wight Bakke, produced other patterns of unemployment, the pattern of 'shock – optimism – pessimism – fatalism' has tended to receive increasing support. In general though, the hypothesis has been illustrated and supported rather than tested and validated. Writers have, I think, tended to look for these patterns among the unemployed they have interviewed and failed to give enough attention to the exceptions or differences that they may encounter.

In some extreme forms the accounts suggest such an inevitability in the successive stages that there can be no escaping them. Once the unemployed has reached the final stage of fatalism, it has become a permanent adjustment to continuing unemployment. Silent toleration appears to be easy acquiescence and acceptance. Some of these studies provide no evidence on the standard of living or the level of income. Given the persistent belief by the public in the adequacy of the many different benefits available today, it is not surprising that the impression is fostered of someone who has settled down to a not too intolerable life on the dole (see section 4.2). One final twist in this argument is that increasing unemployment may actually encourage this belief. The media are very correctly explaining that the present government's attempt to control the money supply is heavily dependent upon its ability to cut the public sector borrowing requirement. One important reason it is so difficult to contain is the increased expenditure on social security due to the rising numbers of unemployed. The very scale of the total social security expenditure on the unemployed reinforces the view of a caring society.

As Richard Harrison pointed out in his detailed review of research into the impact of unemployment for the Department of Employment in 1976, 'the idea of a series of stages may well apply to people in their prime years with a history of steady employment. But the great majority of these workers are amongst the first to find work again. If their unemployment is prolonged, though, it is clear that it brings many people face to face with acute personal dilemmas and fundamental questions about their identity and value to society' (Harrison, 1976, p.340).

For very many unemployed, however, the idea of a fixed pattern of stages does not seem appropriate. In interviews, the two main and contrasting reactions can be summed up by 'I never thought it would happen to me' and 'That's your fate'. It is the very rawness and sharpness of the shock that makes the first pattern much more evident, particularly in the single interview. A man who has never been out of work and has only just been made redundant will often be very eager to talk about the injustice and outrage. The vividness and even bitterness may be all the sharper if he has spent most of his working life with one company and doubts whether he will ever find another job. In some interviews with a man like this, I have had to ask very few questions: he is more than prepared to tell me the full story with very little prompting. Whether shock is followed by optimism or pessimism is likely to depend upon age, health and the level of resources, including past pay and any final settlement. Knowledge of the local labour market and of the demand for any skills he has or the extent of his informal contacts may also be crucial (see section 2.2).

By contrast, the unskilled man in his forties, now in his second or third spell out of work this year, may be laconic to the extent of disconcerting the most experienced interviewers. He realises that he is becoming more vulnerable to unemployment, especially if he is disabled or his health is deteriorating, and he knows that the market is becoming much slacker at the same time. There is little new or different about this time out of work: if he is fortunate in getting back to work, he is aware that it will probably not be long before he becomes unemployed again. The most inept question, such as 'What is it like to be out of work?', which will set the first man vividly talking, may simply elicit a blank or puzzled stare from the second. For him, being out of work is part and parcel of being in that sort of job. He doesn't expect it to change − in the end, the older are always being pushed out by the younger and fitter. But this does not represent a fatalism that accepts continuing unemployment. It is often very much more a reaction to a repetition of unemployment and the uncertainty of the job search.

These are obviously extreme examples, but I have frequently met both types. Now that unemployment has been rising for many months, more of the redundant, especially the older ones, may lose their volubility and simply be numbed by what looks even more like the premature end to their working careers. But this change is by no means evident. Interviewers continue to remark on the almost unbelievable optimism with which men who coped with unemployment a decade ago opt for the attraction of the lump-sum redundancy payment expecting to find work again in a couple of months at the latest.

In between the two extremes there is a wide range of experiences. Very little appears to be known about the impact of unemployment on the married woman. The pressures and tensions she encounters, losing her paid job and 'only' being left her housework, may depend on the extent of her family responsibilities and the need to find employment again quickly − whether to maintain her own independence and career or to restore the family's reduced resources. Tensions and frustration may be all the greater when two members of the same household are out of work. The impact on the school leaver may change dramatically as the weeks stretch into months and many of those who left at the same time find work. His or her fatalism may be much more a matter of accepting the abandonment of previous ambitions and settling for a series of uninteresting but physically demanding dead-end jobs.

For all unemployed people, the level of demand seems particularly important. A skilled man with sound experience and good health may be able to accept the delay until work returns after a seasonal decline because he expects to be taken on again. This is very different from the man made redundant whose skill is no longer needed. Movement between jobs may be a useful way of gaining experience for teenagers without any skills and be a sensible way of coping with the monotony and boredom of many of the jobs available for younger school leavers. But, as Phillips (1973) has said, 'such gains become deadly' when unemployment is high. Employers may prefer to take those straight from school who have not built up what is now seen in a declining labour market as an unstable work record.

The other main factor that I believe affects the reaction to unemployment and influences its impact is the range of resources the unemployed person can command, whether they are economic or social, in terms of family support or help and guidance through colleagues and neighbours. In my view, some of the more psychological analyses have completely overlooked the impact of reduced income on the unemployed and their families. The lack of resources may increase the burden of unemployment and at the same time make it more difficult to escape back to work (see section 2.4).

Very often the impact of unemployment is revealed most clearly in interviews with men now back in work. It is perhaps hardly to be expected that families hard-pushed to cope with the burden of unemployment will tell a complete stranger what loss of work is doing to them, their families, their marriage and their lives. The family tensions and arguments often come out much more vividly in recollection. Men I have often regarded as quite hardened or accustomed to unemployment in my first interview with them when they were out of work, have spoken angrily and with great relief of the hardships, pressures and often unremitting monotony of that time once they are back in work. This is brought out in two interviews with workers made redundant in Newcastle in 1978. Both were in their fifties and had been back at work six months before the interview.

It affected me a lot when I was unemployed. I didn't think I was going to get another job. It was very depressing and got worse the longer I was unemployed. It wasn't so much the money or the way I felt. It was degrading – in the dole office or when people asked me what I was doing. People would say – 'are you still unemployed?' 'Are you not looking for work?' I was looking. It was very degrading. I have worked all my life and got angry. People who have never been unemployed don't know what it is like; they have never experienced it . . . When you are unemployed you are bored, frustrated, and worried, worried sick: at least I was. Of course it is worse for the man who has got a family: he has got responsibilities. So you worry for the wife and the bairns.

The second man had taken a poorer job as a labourer, which he had got through a friend after four months out of work.

When I was unemployed I was very worried: I thought that was it, I didn't expect to get another job. I slept in late until about 11 a.m. I got very bored. Hours in the early afternoon were the worst – hours when I thought that I used to be working. I wasn't ready for retiring yet: I can still work, I wanted to work. I got very jealous of those who were working. My wife is right when she said it affects me *as a man*: it isn't the money so much as the feeling men have. [Newcastle, 1980, p.34]

My impression is that there are more references to humiliation and anger and depression in the comments from those back at work, but fewer references to the importance of income. In the interviews with those out of work, the opposite pattern often emerges. Change of location can also make a difference. I have noticed that interviews in the home, often in front of the family with members joining in, may pick up many of the deprivations that are being experienced at the present time. Interviews with groups of unemployed outside the benefit office or in a pub are often much more focused on work and the loss of it. They also talk more of the job search discussed in the next section.

2.2 THE SEARCH FOR WORK

You meet people and they ask you what you are doing and you say you are unemployed and you know what they are thinking. You can tell yourself that you don't care what they think but deep down it gets you. It always gets you. Sometimes people will say 'you are still not working? You are not trying man. I have got a job. There's plenty of jobs for those who want to work'. But I am trying. [Craftsman redundant for 12 months – Newcastle, 1980, p.36]

One of the greatest ironies in the creation of the mythology of the voluntary unemployed is the success of some in finding work. In a work-oriented society that condemns idleness there is strong encouragement for the successful job-searcher to congratulate himself and play down any element of good fortune. This seems all the more likely to happen when the search has been long and difficult because of the shortage of jobs. Besides, many people do not have to register very long before they are successful in finding a new job. More than 1 in 4 spells of male unemployment lasted less than four days according to a detailed analysis of all spells between June 1971 and 1972 (Stern, 1979, p.69). However, this was a time when unemployment rose quickly but fell equally rapidly; unemployment is now more than twice as high and still rising. Even so, during the high level of unemployment in 1975, the number of unemployed registering for less than four weeks never fell below 180,000.

Many people looking for work find it harder to get a job than they expected. This includes skilled men made redundant in their thirties or forties who generally have much less difficulty in finding work unless their particular skill has become obsolete. When Tress Engineering closed on Tyneside in June 1978, only a third of the redundant workers believed their chances of getting any jobs were poor, although many more had less confidence in being able to get a similar job. But one year later more than one-half had found that looking for work was worse or a lot worse than they had expected, and this included men who had succeeded in getting a new job. Many of the skilled who had been more optimistic initially had been much more shocked by their experience. In total, over a quarter had to change their minds about the type of work they were looking for. Most of the men took the first job they were offered and less than 1 in 5 said they had actually turned down the offer of a job. Most of these were skilled men, half of whom had turned down a job in favour of another that they preferred or because it would have involved moving home. Those without any skill had been much more pessimistic about their chances in the labour market and hardly any had turned down a job offer (Newcastle, 1980).

It is often argued that many unemployed could find work quicker if they did not set their sights too high and were not cushioned by generous or at least high benefits. The evidence for this appears to be largely anecdotal and is not supported by the findings of many surveys over the last fifteen years. One study in 1979 showed that a majority of unemployed men had tended to come from low-paying jobs, but only 3 per cent would be receiving more in benefits than they had previously earned (the average gap was £34 per week). Those who managed to find a new job generally suffered a reduction in earnings but their new take-home pay was still on average £28 more than their benefit income. Those with relatively higher benefits because they had many dependants were generally looking for higher earnings and tended to take longer to find a new job. There was no evidence, however, that they were not looking for work as hard as the others. They put fewer restrictions on the type of job that they would take and had made more job applications than those with low benefit incomes. They were also most likely to be suffering financial hardship (Smith, 1980). The national DHSS Cohort Study (Moylan and Davies, 1980) of men becoming unemployed in the autumn of 1978 also found that there was little if any evidence of the earnings target being set too high.

I have been struck by the sheepishness or defensiveness with which men explain why they have taken a job for a low wage, including one beneath their benefit income. Many see it as a defeat: unlike others, they have neither succeeded in getting back to work quickly on their own terms nor had the guts to hold out for the type of job they used to have. Taking lower pay often means accepting a poorer job with less status and requiring less of their skill – it means a lowering of standards that may be never regained.

In examining the job-search and its intensity, one has to take account of the differences among those out of work. Most importantly of all, the demand for workers in some occupations is very much lower than in others. Opportunities for unskilled workers are particularly limited. In September 1980, when unemployment had been rising and vacancies dropping so steadily, there were 162 people registered as general labourers for every job known to the employment service. The average number registered unemployed for all other occupations was ten. The chances also varied very greatly by region, and an analysis within these would probably have shown even greater variation in job opportunity. Workers also differ in their previous experience at finding work and the resources they can bring to bear. In some occupations there are traditional patterns of finding employment — for example through the Seaman's Pool or the local Sheet-metal Workers Union. Some companies only take on people through the job shop while others prefer people to 'exercise their own initiative' and call at the factory gates.

The atmosphere is very different when there is only a temporary lull in employment. Tradesmen in the shipyards may expect a recall when work returns. There are certain known places to look for notification of jobs besides the job shop and an efficient work-seeker who intends to stay within a certain range of jobs may save himself the tedious and depressing trudge from factory to factory that generally still has to be made by those without a skill. This can change very quickly when there is a more general slump. Even in good times the older unemployed man whose health is deteriorating or skill becoming obsolete may have to turn to other ways of looking for work.

Amongst the great majority of those I have interviewed it has become very evident that there is no single 'right way' to look for work and what is seen as luck has often tended to dominate the job-search, especially for the unskilled. This helps to account for the fatalistic attitude expressed by many men without skills.

> I am a great fatalist — whatever comes along, that is your fate. Oh, but you have got to go and look for work, you have got to push yourself. Perhaps you will be going to one place and there won't be work — at another there will be. That's your fate.

This has been brought home to me in interviews time and time again.

> I got my last job myself — not that I can say I got it by looking for it. I had been down to the yards looking and had no luck. On the way back I stopped to talk to some men working on the corner just over there [he nodded across the road from his house] and I got taken on.

For these men there was no spur of efficiency, no premium on effort, and the pub or the betting shop could be as good a place to find work as the factory gate or the job shop. One hot tip for a job may be dud; the place was filled weeks ago. Another time this may lead to a job. 'I don't know what to say to him when he comes back in', said one wife of a semi-skilled worker who had been three months out of work, 'I don't know why he does it.' Good fortune in finding work is acknowledged, but this type of success only confirms one's own inability to dominate and overcome the situation. One apprentice plumber eventually found work.

> It wasn't easy, not easy at all. I wanted a trade, something I could learn that would be useful not just any old job. My father has a trade and I wanted to have a trade too. I looked around went to all the building sites, in town. I even went to one building site 7 weeks in a row. Even then I never got a start. It was through a neighbour I got the job I'm in now. He told me they were looking for apprentices, so I went down next day and was told to start the next week. [Gow and McPherson, 1980]

The role of the family and friends in helping the unemployed to find work is very important and is obscured by much research that simply asks those out of work what methods they are using to find a job. Without prompting, few will think to mention their family or friends. But this of course does not mean that a relative or friend who hears of a suitable job may not follow it up or speak for the unemployed to the employer. Parents, for example, have often asked their employers about possible jobs for their children and vice versa. Informal contacts are still so important in finding and keeping work that the unemployed often say 'it's who you know, not what you know' that determines the chances of re-employment. Over half of the men who found work after the Tress redundancy in Newcastle did so through informal contacts. This was much more common amongst men who were likely to have greater difficulty in finding work. Older workers or those without skills found particularly severe problems in an area where unemployment among men had been at least 10 per cent for many years. Yet four men, all over 50 and without a skill, found jobs within three months — all, significantly, through relatives working for their new employers (Newcastle, 1980, p.12). Similarly in North Shields, an unskilled man of 63, the oldest I met who found another job after being made redundant, was taken on by his son's employer: 'he told my lad when he knew the timberworks had closed "if he's as good a worker as you are . . ." '.

The informal method has advantages to both employer and job-seeker. The employee-contact has virtually approved the job for his unemployed friend and told him its attractions and faults and at the same time effectively given a reference on his friend to both the employer and his work colleagues. The fact that a relative or friend spoke for him may well lead a man to put up with much more than he might otherwise do in the initial, often difficult, settling-in period. The employer also knows this and so may be more willing to take him on. Contacts and the chance to vet informally on both sides therefore play a valuable role in bringing job and job-seeker together quickly and efficiently. Their importance is all the greater in unskilled and less skilled jobs, although in taking on apprentices employers also often give preference to the families of their own workers or those they have spoken for.

But any practice that discriminates in favour of some will leave others more disadvantaged. Those who do not have good contacts and are not established or accepted in the local community become more dependent on their own unassisted efforts or the help of the job shop. In North Tyneside we found that this worked against men in their forties and fifties living by themselves and with no regular family contacts. Their poverty reinforced their isolation, cutting them off from the main source of jobs (North Tyneside CDP, 1978). This may well help to account for the higher rate of unemployment among those who are single or no longer married.

Immigrant and ethnic minority groups are also likely to find these patterns of recruitment working against their attempts to find work until they have become established and accepted in the local community. Many careers officers or job centre staff do not appreciate that this places an additional premium on their own efforts to help 'outsiders' find work. By continuing to use this established and accepted practice, employers and others have the effect of discriminating against, for example, black school leavers. The higher unemployment rate among West Indian as opposed to Asian teenagers may be partly an effect of this pattern of recruitment combined with the differing occupational and industrial structure of the two groups. There are more Asians than West Indians in employing positions, such as small businessmen and shopkeepers, so that there is likely to be a larger pool of jobs known among the Asian community in the same informal way. And, as the number of vacancies falls further short of the numbers looking for work, one might expect that a greater proportion of jobs will be filled through informal contacts.

Higher unemployment brings a marked reduction in opportunities for those who lack both skills and contacts, and enormously increases their frustration and tension. In the last resort the nature of the job-search is decided by whether the employer or the unemployed is looking harder for the other. When employers are more concerned with finding the essential worker to complete the work team, their attitude and behaviour are very different from those who dismiss the idea of putting up notices outside factory gates with jobs for labourers because 'we would be deluged if we did. We only advertise skilled jobs and tell the job shop about unskilled vacancies'.

2.3   THE ORGANISATION OF THE UNEMPLOYED

Given the isolation, boredom, monotony and general emptiness of life described by those who remain out of work for a long time, some means of promoting closer and easier contact among the unemployed would seem valuable. Of course, the places where they are brought together most of all are the job centre and the benefit office — many new registrants, including students or journalists in search of copy, have commented on the general silence of the slow shuffle forward with the majority appearing to be very withdrawn. The exceptions, chatting or calling out to others in the queue as they come in, generally seem to be neighbours or workers from the same company. But the atmosphere generally discourages contact amongst the unemployed. The way in which the very need to compete for the work available and the isolating experience of being out of work tend to set one person apart from another has worked against organisation of the unemployed. But from time to time, as unemployment has hit particularly hard at one community or one company, there has been some effort at organisation. With the rise of unemployment in the early 1960s, which was particularly severe in the more depressed areas, clubs and associations sprang up in a number of areas only to disappear when the initiators themselves returned to work. And this is a key problem for any organisation of the unemployed — that the most active and competent organisers are also likely to be people most skilful at obtaining work. The exception will be the organiser who is so militant that he becomes blacklisted or unacceptable to employers.

The sudden upsurge of claimants' unions in the early 1970s included many with unemployed members (Rose, 1973). Some of these were trade unionists who started to run the groups along conventional union branch lines and often clashed with others who wanted a less structured group. The longest lasting of all these has been the Claimants and Unemployed Workers Union of Barnsley established by Joe Kenyon, a disabled ex-miner and trade union negotiator in his fifties, although it has largely survived as a one-man operation, providing advice on benefits and welfare rights and maintaining a flow of leaflets and broadsheets (for an account of part of the work, see Gould and Kenyon, 1972, especially Chapter 13).

Probably the most significant organisation has been the Centre for the Unemployed set up with the help of Newcastle Trades Council in 1978. Despite problems of funding and cuts in grants from the local authority, which are said to have been the result of deliberate political intervention, the Centre has survived, in part with help from the Manpower Services

Commission STEP programme. It has provided somewhere for many unemployed to meet and has done much to organise public support and distribute information on unemployment to counter the attacks on benefits and scroungerphobia (see NCU, 1980a, b). Very much encouraged by its example, groups or centres have been set up elsewherc including Middlesbrough, Stockton, Edinburgh, Kings Lynn and Scunthorpe. In other cities there has been considerable resistance from bodies such as the trades councils and other groups to support any such venture, which has been dismissed as exploitation of the unemployed by political extremists. This of course may be possible – in one area the only significant organised effort was to recruit unemployed for an anti-Nazi League demonstration some 50 miles away, and there was little attempt to promote activities on behalf of the unemployed in the local area or to advise them of their rights or anything else. The TUC is now encouraging unions and trades councils to support unemployed centres (TUC, 1980) and in South Wales has secured a government grant to promote these. How effective it will be in overcoming the reluctance of many trade unions and trades councils we do not know, but the absence of any lobby or pressure-group for the unemployed has been a major obstacle to presenting their case and a more sustained and widespread critique of the scrounger mythology. This is all the more important because many union members who are hard pressed by high rates and the standard rate of tax on below-average earnings are all the more prone to accept stories of affluence and comfort on the dole without the daily stress of having to earn a living.

2.4   POVERTY OUT OF WORK

'One of the enduring myths about unemployment is that its link with poverty has been broken' (Walker, 1981). This is not only a very persistent myth but a very powerful one, which allows or even encourages the rest of society to accept higher levels of unemployment more easily. Benefits are so generous and numerous in the welfare state, it is argued, that being out for work for a few weeks or months does not bring the hardships that it did in the 1930s. Besides, wages are

much higher and many families have two adult wage-earners
so they are much better prepared to cope with unemployment. Even people who discount stories of scroungers, dole-
dodgers and unemployables may find reassurance from these
beliefs as unemployment continues upward. There is a world
recession, and inflation is severe for those in work. If unemployment is part of the cost of getting the economy back on
its feet, this can be endured if the benefits available can take
the sting out of worklessness. After all, that is exactly what
they were intended to do. The ideal of 'the welfare state'
encompassed the belief that benefits should be sufficient to
keep those dependent on them out of poverty and give enough
support to save them from having to take the first job that
came along, however bad its pay and conditions.

When the sharply rising numbers of unemployed mean
more people suffering more and longer spells out of work, it
is particularly important to examine the financial impact.
Despite the increasing number of benefits, the many changes
and what have now become annual upratings of benefits, the
main finding has remained depressingly the same in every
study of unemployment since the war that I have examined.
One detailed survey in Coventry, Hammersmith and Newcastle
in 1971 concluded that 'the majority of the unemployed
were living . . . on what can be described as no more than
subsistence incomes' (Hill *et al.,* 1973). This picture was
supported by a national survey in 1973 that found that the
costs remained 'substantial for all groups' and the unemployed
'were by no means compensated by the level of social benefits
received' (Daniel, 1974). Official analyses show the much
greater risk of poverty among those out of work for three
months or more compared with households where the main
wage-earner was in work. During the high unemployment of
1976 the unemployed were twenty-one times more likely to
be in poverty.

The combination of low pay with previous periods of unemployment and sickness leaves few of those out of work
with any resources apart from state benefits after a month. In
the national Cohort Study 7 out of 10 men still unemployed
after a month reported that they had 'no unearned income
and no income from a wife's earnings *and* savings of less than

£500' (SBC, 1980, p.34). Those who report little or no financial hardship have not only received the highest state benefits but have generally also been supported by private and state redundancy payments in a lump sum, severance pay and payments in lieu of notice. In the Cohort Study, the total receiving any of these payments came to less than 10 per cent. The majority therefore have to manage on incomes around supplementary benefit level. In particular, the inadequacy of the rates to support those with children has been emphasised time and again by the Supplementary Benefits Commission and has even been acknowledged by the present government. 'I accept', said the Minister for Social Security to a House of Commons Standing Committee in February 1980, 'that the provision for children under the Supplementary Benefits scheme is not good enough, has never been good enough, and will not be good enough following the [review] changes' (SBC, 1980, p.84 – for a discussion of the effect of the review changes see section 4.1).

The inadequacy of the standard of living possible on supplementary benefits is documented very clearly in official research carried out in October 1974 (at that time the value of benefits in relation to average net earnings for a married couple appears slightly higher than it is today). Only 1 in 20 of the unemployed on supplementary benefit said that they were 'managing quite well' and most were single men. The majority of families with two or more children said that they were 'getting into difficulties'. On measure after measure of deprivation and disadvantage, families with children were found to be worse off, particularly if unemployment had been prolonged. Most people had to cut back on their expenses, but there were far more economies amongst families. The larger families were much more likely to be living in over-crowded accommodation and to have used up any savings. The greater poverty of families was also shown by their 'un-met needs' in terms, for example, of the clothing, bedding and household equipment that the Supplementary Benefits Commission set out in their guidelines. 'Three-quarters of the men with children did not have one complete change of clothing, a warm coat and two pairs of shoes' and families as a whole tended to be very poorly clothed (Clark, 1978).

Subsequent research has produced more evidence of acute financial hardship, particularly as unemployment becomes prolonged. Enough for 'existence rather than living' was the conclusion of the Manpower Services Commission's own detailed study of people out of work for over a year in the middle of 1979 (Colledge and Bartholomew, 1980). Another survey in the same year reported that the most frequent answer by the unemployed to what was the worst thing about being out of work emphasised the financial problems. Half the men had fallen behind on regular payments, such as rent, rates, mortgages and fuel bills (Smith, 1980).

The lack of any significant improvement over time and the higher incomes of those in work was brought out very clearly in much smaller studies in North Shields in 1963/4 and 1975/6. In both studies the number of unemployed men with weekly incomes more than 40 per cent above the basic supplementary benefits level was very small — only 3 out of 92 in the first study and 7 out of 100 in the second study. Most were single men living with their parents who had been out of work for only a fairly short period. The second study enabled a comparison to be made with men in work in the same area, and 9 out of 10 employed men had incomes above this level. The main difference between the two groups of unemployed was that the abolition of the wage-stop regulation in mid-1975 meant that fewer of the unemployed were pulled far below supplementary benefits level in the second study. But in both studies families with children were likely to be the worst off.

The wretched position of families deserves emphasis because of the particularly vicious circle in which they are caught. Many of their needs cannot be deferred, and extra heating for very young babies and winter shoes and coats for growing children all bite into the weekly budget. One family where the father had had very little work after contracting tuberculosis fifteen years ago ate particularly poorly. The parents never had any breakfast, and had just a sandwich at lunch and some form of hot meal in the evening — with no supper, they added. They found Thursday and Friday before benefit arrived the most difficult days on which to manage. As I got to know them, I discovered how very frugally they lived. Over the years they had clearly put a lot of thought into budgeting, buying savings stamps for heatings costs and so on. Most of their clothing was obtained from the Nearly New shops and charity sales. These more deprived groups are all the more likely to get caught in the trap of having to pay more to purchase clothing and other essentials through clubs and local stores with high interest rates. 'This put further pressure on a weekly income already tightly stretched to cover basic necessities' and this state of chronic poverty became even more acute as unemployment lengthened. Not surprisingly therefore, one-third of the families who had three or more children had debts of £50 or more (Clark, 1978). Yet families, especially large ones, are the group that most people in work believe to be best protected, if not cushioned, by the bounty of the welfare state. Many unemployed families are acutely aware of this, mentioning, for example, fights that children have got into at school: 'his dad said they were supporting people like us'.

The combination of a reduced budget and more contact between husband and wife enforced by the lack of daily work routine has been shown to cause increasing tension within families, especially when relations may not have been too strong in the first place. Many men report that the most frequent rows are over money and children, and studies report disturbing evidence of violence and family break-ups linked to unemployment (Colledge and Bartholomew, 1980, and J.M. Hill, 1978). There are also increasing reports from groups such as the Samaritans, NSPCC and many working in the social services (Popay, 1981).

Observing the pressures and strains that poverty and prolonged unemployment place on many families, my own research has made me much more conscious of the many ways the double impact wears them down and turns them in on themselves. The silent endurance of deprivation and rejection does not make headlines, and is astonishingly often dismissed as apathy or lack of will. Going without what most of society has come to expect is a daily burden. It may be particularly upsetting for unemployed parents at a child's birthday or Christmas, but it is a constant and very undramatic struggle. Often the extended family will take some of the strain, feeding children some evenings or weekends, keeping up their pocket money and paying for winter shoes and clothing. The poverty of many families out of work would be very much sharper if retired grandparents did not help and so reduce their own limited resources.

In many ways, however, poverty is an isolating experience. Joe Kenyon has noticed in his work with claimants how people become 'locked into poverty' so that their home becomes a prison. When they had a job, it was somewhere that most were glad to return to; but poor and out of work they find their home is 'a mouth that eats up' their money before they start to buy food for themselves. In their attempts to cope, they cut themselves off from others. The Supplementary Benefits Commission has defined poverty today as 'a standard of living so low that it excludes and isolates people from the rest of the community'. Poverty-caused isolation deprives people of the social contacts that not only help them to survive the crisis but may also be their main way of finding work and so their only chance of escaping poverty.

Given the persistent evidence of poverty in the surveys of the unemployed, even official ones, it is tempting to imagine some malevolent conspiracy of silence. While much of the hostility encouraged by stories about scroungers and the work-shy may play an important part in distracting public attention, there are many other factors that serve to disguise or divert attention from the financial problems of the unemployed. Ironically, one of these factors is the experience of many short-term unemployed who may receive substantial income tax rebates on top of their earnings-related supplement, insurance benefit and any lump-sum payments from their employer for redundancy, severance or in lieu of notice. They may dislike the experience and be glad to be back in work, but clearly they have not endured any poverty.

It is important, however, not to slip into the complacent belief that the return to work always means an escape from poverty. One of the most disturbing findings from Peter Townsend's study of poverty in the United Kingdom was that poverty continued to exist 'for the much larger number than the currently out of work of those who experienced spells of unemployment (however short) in the recent past', because they had either found poorly paid jobs or 'had become sick, or unemployed again' (Townsend, 1979, p.614). Nearly 2 out of 5 households in which the head had been unemployed for ten or more weeks in the previous year were in or on the margins of poverty according to the state poverty standard in 1968/9. (Section 1.2 drew attention to the persisting concentration of unemployment among the poorly paid.)

So far, I have been concerned to show that the link between poverty and unemployment has not been broken. But concentration on this aspect alone may reinforce long-held assumptions about what is a matter for concern during unemployment. Unemployment may not mean poverty to many of those out of work but it nonetheless represents a significant loss and deprivation. High unemployment makes it unwise to risk time 'looking around' for a better offer; many more people experience only a short time out of work but go back to lower-paying jobs. Older workers who are fortunate enough to get another job at all are particularly likely to go back to a job with less status and reward, and this seems true in any occupation or profession. Even if they return to the same level, they have often missed the next step up the ladder and from then on find they are competing with younger, better trained colleagues.

The combination of material and career loss may be much more significant than people care to admit or maybe realise during their unemployment. In detailed interviews with husbands and wives in a sub-sample of her survey of redundant managers, Jean Hartley found only one family that said they had a much reduced standard of living and, in general, there was not much evidence of 'cutting back' in a major way (Hartley, 1978). What became evident on closer examination was that managers often used their savings or obtained credit rather than change their life-style while they were out of work, hoping that they would soon find a job. 'Several were already seriously in debt and one manager cashed in his pension . . . the majority of managers expressed anxiety about their savings; when to use them, how much to use before changing their job plans, what to do when savings ran out.' In his interviews with professional and managerial men, Robert Slater found (1975) that families also drew on 'potential

savings'. These are savings families would have made had the
man not been unemployed and for the first few months they
used up these before touching any capital — one example
would be wives' earnings normally saved for special expenditure on the home or towards a move to a better one. It is
also very common for the unemployed to cash in insurance
policies with the treble loss of continuing protection, a poor
surrender value and a much higher premium if a new policy is
taken out later. Similarly, families selling a car during unemployment cannot wait for the best price and receive less than
if they are trading it in.

Maintaining your current standard of living and risking
future financial problems may be a small price to pay when it
maintains your self-respect and confidence and makes it more
likely that you will get the job you want. 'Do not take the
first job you are offered' is the advice given by those counselling redundant executives. 'Think positively and aim high'
(*Sunday Times,* 13 December 1980). Most people approve
these strategies and recognise the importance and difficulty
of keeping up one's confidence in the face of continuing
unemployment. Yet many of the same people are often very
critical of the refusal of any job offer and of what they see as
the inappropriate spending or mis-spending of the poorer
unemployed with whom they are less able to identify. In one
survey I asked unemployed families if there were any things
they spent money on which they felt they should not. The
wife of one particularly poor family of four, living in two
very dilapidated rooms, replied: 'What, to cheer us up, do
you mean? Oh yes, sometimes Jack would get his dole on a
Friday afternoon and on his way home get pasties, bacon and
eggs. We couldn't really afford it, but we were so sick of it
all.' I have mentioned this in discussions and it has been used
to support the view that the poor obviously need more advice
on how to budget and manage.

This is a particularly good example of the ways in which
social familiarity or distance help to influence how we per-
ceive the problems and strategies of others. Social distance
reduces our ability, quite simply, to see the needs and difficulties of those furthest removed from our own daily lives, as
Victorian commentators on the poverty of 'Darkest England'

pointed out (cf. Keating, 1976). When the problem is concentrated disproportionately, as is unemployment, among the poorer and less powerful members of our society the danger of the failure to recognise the need for action is all the greater. It is one of the less evident of the 'hidden injuries of class' (Sennett and Cobb, 1973).

CHAPTER THREE

Who are the Unemployed?

3.1 MASS REDUNDANCIES IN A COLD CLIMATE

The five groups discussed in this chapter have been chosen to give depth to the more general picture of the experience of unemployment presented in chapter 2.

Redundancies increased at a dramatic rate in 1980 to create yet another depressing economic record in post-war Britain. By the end of October 1980 notified redundancies had climbed to a total of 384,400. So the first ten months of 1980 took us 14 per cent above the total for the whole of 1971, the previous highest year. As *The Times* reported in September 1980, 'a wholesale shakeout of labour is in progress right across the industrial board' with evidence 'of longterm job-shedding in consumer industries where the recession is only just starting to bite' (*The Times*, 24 September 1980). A month later, 'industrial leaders are expressing anxiety that job cuts are now starting to deprive them of staff who will be needed once the recession ends' including many white-collar staff (*The Times*, 22 October 1980). In November the list of firms announcing redundancies and reductions of 100 or more jobs was double that for October — a dismal roll-call of 107 companies including many of Britain's leading manufacturers in what have been seen as the new, export-producing and wealth-creating industries. The report was tersely pessimistic: 'There is no sign that the bottom has yet been reached.' Despite some hopes from the reduction in interest rates earlier in the week, 'all the industrial indicators . . . signal that the shakeout in manufacturing industry will continue until well into the new year' (*The Times*, 26 November 1980).

In those three months, industries that lost most jobs were iron and steel, motor vehicle manufacturing, other metal goods and construction. Together with clothing, in October 1980 these contributed about one-third of all the official notifications. The 1980 total may well turn out to be more than three times above 1979. In some industries the reduction in the number of jobs over a longer period of time has been very substantial indeed — for example coalmining, ship-building, agriculture, textiles, railways and the production of railway stock, and iron and steel. The visible impact of the steep decline in employment in industries such as these has been all the greater because they have been concentrated in particular areas where they were the dominant industry for many decades. Many of them were the growth leaders of the first industrial revolution and the history of the working class and the development of British trade unions is very much part of their own rise and fall.

The reduction of jobs in a company or industry may not in itself be a symptom of national decline, however great the loss to those whose lives have been shaped and dominated by that industry. The extreme examples are those in the essential industries where production was so vital during the war that military conscription did not apply. Some, made redundant by closures of the mines in Cumberland, West Durham and Northumberland in the 1950s and 1960s, had never worked outside the same pit since leaving school forty or fifty years before. In many of these villages nearly all other employment was serving mining directly, or else indirectly in meeting the consumer demands of miners and their families (Bulmer, 1978).

In 1980, signs of regeneration were little evident in an economic climate that even ICI, one of Britain's leading manufacturers and exporters, described as not so much 'bracing' as liable to cause us to 'freeze to death'.

Investment in the current climate has collapsed. Increases in bank borrowing are not to finance new projects but to provide working capital. 'Spending on machinery is merely to keep it running not to improve facilities' was how one industrial expert described the approach of management. [*Financial Times* Survey on Birmingham and West Midlands, 26 November 1980]

An increasing number of industrialists now fear that even an economic recovery will not raise demand sufficiently to stimulate and maintain real growth in our manufacturing capacity. Certainly the growth of new, more advanced and more competitive industries has been very much less than was needed.

Redundancy payments were originally introduced in the optimistic days of the mid-1960s to remove the resistance of workers, trade unions and employers to cutting out unproductive jobs. It was hoped that this would encourage redeployment and speed up productive growth by overcoming tendencies to labour immobility and overmanning. Today it appears that the redundancy payments scheme is simply being used to cope with a cash crisis and other problems of our current recession rather than to lay the basis for future efficiency. In a changing society, workers and whole communities may be paying the cost of the larger nation's progress. The charge upon a just society must be to ensure that all that can possibly be done is done to reduce the costs and suffering that are borne privately. The growth and development of compensation for the loss of a job through redundancy payments must therefore be seen as an important advance towards this more just society.

At present the maximum payment under the state-sponsored scheme to which employers and state contribute is £3,600. How much is paid depends on a formula weighted in favour of older workers receiving higher pay who have been longer with the same employer. To earn the maximum you will need to be over 40 and earning at least £120 a week with fifteen years' service with that one employer. A younger worker would need more years of service. Considerable publicity has been given to some of the largest lump sums, so it is important to note that the average payment was only £874 in 1979. And by no means everyone made redundant benefits under the state-organised scheme, let alone collects another grant from the employer. For instance, there is no entitlement at all to payment from the state scheme until you are over 18 and have been with the same employer for at least two years. One attraction of the lump-sum payment is that it is free of tax up to £10,000. Above that there are various devices such as top-slicing to reduce tax, which can often be avoided completely up to £20,000. In effect this is a considerable tax subsidy to those with large private payments and good tax advisers.

For many manual workers, especially perhaps older ones, £2–3,000 is a substantial 'nest egg'. Some talk of 'going for their redundancy' in their early sixties much as one might talk of a long-service medal. It may certainly allow a freedom of spending that workers may never have experienced before. Well aware of the declining resources of retirement, they know that they will never have such a chance again. There are reports that pubs outside redundancy-prone factories on Clydeside are changing hands for 'astronomical sums' but such speculation may only prosper while the speed and size of redundancies require the production-line farewell ceremonies, with as many as fifteen sharing the limelight, that Alan Road (1980) observed in Port Talbot: 'A few pints, a brief valediction and a performance by a stripper have brought down the curtain on many a career in recent weeks.' However, even the celebrations or the wake tend to be short. A lot of the spending is very much more instrumental: stocking up against retirement, replacing or adding to household equipment and furnishings, paying off all or part of the mortgage or buying a council house. Banks have set up 'portakabins' at larger closures, such as Port Talbot, to provide advice on investing the payments.

One of the points that is overlooked in much of the discussion of 'three-month millionaires' is that the redundancy payment may be only one part, and a small one, of the lump sum received by a worker on leaving a company. When Tress Engineering closed in Newcastle in 1978, the average total lump sum was £1,600 with 1 in 9 of the workers receiving more than £2,500. But the redundancy payment part of this averaged only £650. Another £350 was severance pay agreed with the company, but for most workers the largest payment was in lieu of notice – some thirteen weeks gross pay – totalling £900 for many of them. This was because the firm decided to stop production immediately and so failed to give the workers the statutory ninety-day notification required when the number of jobs lost reached three figures. This payment disqualified the men from claiming unemployment insurance benefit for thirteen weeks during the period covered by their notice. So the largest part of the final handshake was intended for living expenses over three months, and this indeed was how almost three-quarters said they used the whole lump sum. 1 in 4 paid off existing debts, 1 in 4 spent the money on a holiday and 1 in 7 used it to buy a car; only four of the 193 interviewed put the money towards buying a house or flat and only one to starting a business (Newcastle, 1980, p. 25). Similarly at the BSC redundancy in Port Talbot, some of the best-paid and longest-serving workers could receive 'a stainless steel handshake of £17,000', but the guarantee of almost two years on 90 per cent wages was what made 'parting such sweet sorrow' for many of them — at least in the short run. And once again there could be no entitlement to unemployment benefit during this period.

The redundancy payments themselves are not dependent on the ex-worker remaining unemployed. They were never intended to support a worker during unemployment but to compensate him for the loss of security and seniority and other benefits he may have built up in the previous job. This form of lump-sum redundancy settlement is much more common in Britain than many other countries. It is worth emphasising that it is an indication of the extent to which we have let our anxieties about the impact of unemployment slip that we now tend to accept that lump-sum payments are working because they are taking the sting out of unemployment, at least for an initial period. But their success in achieving even this depends on the level of commitments families have. Many have recently bought a house or have begun to rely on two wages coming in to build an extension or improve their home, buy a car or just plan for a better holiday. In some districts or small towns two people in the same family have lost their jobs with the closure of the major employer, and the chance of both finding work quickly is slight.

All the different payments, including unemployment benefit, may not enable the same standard of living and commitments to be kept up for very long. Nearly 2 out of 5 workers from the Tress closure had to cut back after only a short period out of work, and the proportion rose to 4 out of 5 among those with as much as six months out of work (Newcastle, 1980, p. 25). For many there is very little protection from a redundancy because they are being paid off for the second or third time and are entitled to little, if any, payment. They are particularly vulnerable on the 'last-in first-out' basis, even when the whole company or section is not being closed down.

Many redundant workers move from one job to another without any period of unemployment in between, and still receive their payments. But there is worrying evidence that the system of compensation is encouraging the longer employed and so older workers to volunteer for redundancy. Ill-informed and over-optimistic about their chances of re-employment, they are likely to discover very quickly how harshly the labour market treats the older unemployed. Many who chose redundancy from Chrysler Linwood said they later regretted their decision. Several recent studies have found a surprisingly high proportion of workers becoming redundant who have had very much more difficulty than they expected in finding a new job. I have already described in section 2.2 how difficult it was for the workers from Tress to find work: 1 in 3 were still out of work at the end of the year. In general, redundant workers are taking much longer to find jobs than in years of lower unemployment, and older workers are experiencing particular difficulty (MacLeod, 1979, pp. 76–7). There appears to be increasing awareness of this problem: at one company recently in a depressed area workers asked for the closure to be brought forward by two months to enable them to look for work before competition from other workers being made redundant made the search for work even more difficult (*The Times*, 8 December, 1980).

Even when workers are successful in returning to work, they often have to settle for less satisfying jobs in terms of pay, status, conditions and security. The large firms with the major pay-offs are often the main employers in the area, generally offering the best wages. Any new job involves a cost in reduced pay and status to a worker who has been among the elite of the local labour force. The casualties from the massive mining, steel, heavy engineering, shipbuilding and railway-workshop redundancies have all tended to suffer this double reduction.

The full impact of a redundancy is not of course simply

measured by the experience of those made redundant, although some of the studies leave one with that impression. The jobs from which the workers were paid off are removed from the labour market and there can be no assumption that an appropriate number of new jobs will be created to absorb the new job-seekers. When unemployment is high or rising, it is all the more necessary to consider the extent to which the newly redundant job-seekers displace those already looking for work. This means that many unemployed get pushed back in the queue and so are likely to be out of work longer. Since employers use length of unemployment as a rough rule of thumb in choosing between applicants, the impact of a redundancy may fall heavily on many already out of work. Thus, the great majority of workers made redundant in Dundee in 1977–8 by NCR and Sidlaw Industries, the largest British jute manufacturer, gained their new jobs at the expense of others looking for work, whether they were already unemployed or were hoping to change jobs or to enter the labour market. Probably no more than one-twentieth of the jobs could not, in the view of the new employers, have been filled by job-seekers already available before the redundancies. It is estimated that the effect of the 1000 redundancies will have extended the length of unemployment among those already out of work by a minimum of over four months (Scottish EPD, 1980).

A major redundancy may affect not only other job-seekers but the whole community. If the company closing is the main employer, it may virtually create a ghost town. The picture of new mobile industries rushing in to absorb the experienced labour force is only appropriate when business is booming and the shortage of labour is sufficient to attract both private and public funds for retraining. The location of much of the traditional industry that is now shaking out so much labour is also much less attractive to many new and growing industries. Secondly, in a declining economy, even the reduction of output by a major company will mean cutbacks and often closures in the smaller firms that supply it. When the suppliers have moved or settled close to cut transport costs, the resulting cutbacks will be a second blow to the local economy and will only increase the multiplier effect from the first redundancy, which is likely to be all the greater in small or isolated communities. The loss of employment will mean a reduction in spending power and so a drop in demand in the local shops and for local services. In Consett the effect may include an increase in the rates of 9p in the pound to make up for the lost BSC contribution or else a reduction in a range of public services. It will also probably mean an increasing number of closures and bankruptcies as local businesses and shops close down. The scale of this is greatly understated by the bankruptcy figures because small shopkeepers tend to sell rather than go bankrupt when they run into difficulties. However, in a depressed area where shops are frequently changing hands, the range and quality of goods available steadily deteriorate before the shops become boarded up.

With major closures the impact may be harsh for those who have not yet entered the labour force. With 6,000 steel jobs going in Port Talbot, one comprehensive schoolteacher expected half the pupils to have unemployed parents in 1981. In addition to all the other family pressures, the generation of school leavers who have grown up expecting a job at British Steel through their parents will now be looking for other work, competing with the increasing flood of school leavers as well as those who have been looking for a permanent job for over a year. There were 500 applications for four apprenticeships at a nearby oil-refinery in 1980. Similarly, the MP for Consett reported that 'there were only 8 advertised vacancies for 1,400 school leavers in the town' in the summer of 1980 when BSC closed its steelworks there and paid off 3,700 workers, despite the fact that this particular operation had been making a profit. The complete closure had, as is often the case, been preceded by earlier cutbacks: the plate-mill was closed in the previous winter with 420 redundancies. The blow was all the greater because the steelworks had dominated the local economy for 140 years. In a classic company town, the Consett Iron Company had owned the shops, the houses and the collieries as well as the steelworks. Dependence upon the steel industry had been further increased in recent years by the swift decline of mining with a loss of some 17,000 jobs (Road, 1980).

Over the last decade there have been many attempts by workers and unions to fight proposed redundancies. The most famous or notorious include the struggles of Jimmy Reid and the Upper Clyde workers, Lucas Aerospace and Meriden Triumph. In general, there has been very limited success and often a great deal of frustration and tension between the workers of a particular company and local and regional trade union officials (Dey, 1979). Often the achievement has been to gain some extra time or additional compensation rather than complete avoidance of the closure. It is too early to say whether the employers' withdrawal of a possible 600 redundancies at Gardners Diesels near Manchester will be of long-term benefit in the present economic climate. It was said that after a seven-week occupation of a factory by workers the company was caught between them and the pressing demands of customers (*Labour Weekly*, 28 November 1980).

The size of the basic state redundancy payment together with an additional sum offered by employers has generally served to weaken the willingness of a sufficient number of employees to resist the planned closures, as at Tress in Newcastle. Many may also be influenced by several months on short time and reduced pay. In a deteriorating economy, they fear that the whole company may be closed, in which case they might expect to receive only their basic redundancy payment, or at least not as generous a settlement. Those with less confidence of finding a new job quickly may well be anxious that their chances would be much reduced if the whole plant is closed down. Resistance is likely to be considerably less successful when the number of closures is high and increasing. Employers, and work colleagues, are very much less open to persuasion that the economy will improve without further crises for the company.

Employers' attitudes to paying off workers can vary considerably. The chairman and managing director of a drop forge firm in the West Midlands which had been founded by his father sixty-five years ago was found dead with 'his head crushed under a 30 cwt. power hammer'. He had made 50 of the 180 workers redundant and left a note 'explaining how depressed he was about the recession and the redundancies'

(*The Guardian*, 28 November 1980). Many employers do all they can to avoid redundancies and pride themselves on their reputation as stable employers, although the importance of this in maintaining prestige with fellow employers has probably never been as great as it has been in, for example, Sweden (Sorrentino, 1980, p. 205). Others are taking advantage of the recession to force workers to accept changes with the threat of redundancies: 'We don't need consultation now'. There is talk of 'a new realism' on the part of workers and management (*The Times*, 8 December 1980). This is also appearing in the tougher handling of redundancies.

Some have threatened to withdraw the offer of an additional payment unless there is full cooperation from the workers and this has often meant considerable overtime working in the last few weeks. Others have proposed extra payments above the state scheme provided that enough voluntary redundancies can be found. This is particularly likely to encourage colleague pressures on older workers to withdraw, even when these recognise that they will find it much more difficult to obtain another job. Reports are increasing of bitter separations between employer and employee, and it is clear that some quite major employers have little interest in maintaining goodwill within the community since they are leaving it for good.

Studies of the unemployed have shown that only a very small minority have received redundancy payments in their present spell out of work (Moylan and Davies, 1980; see also Daniel, 1974). Those made redundant are likely to be more successful in obtaining work when this is available. But the number who have been paid off and remain out of work is bound to increase when one hundred or more companies are having to close every week and few firms are taking on workers. There are others too, losing their jobs because of closures, who have not worked long enough with that company to gain any redundancy payment.

While it is important not to confuse redundancy with the wider problem of unemployment, the two issues are intimately related, as this chapter has shown. The far-reaching effects of redundancies may be considerable. Even if those made redundant do not remain unemployed, they may still fail to regain the careers and standard of living they previously had. In addition, the impact of redundancy on a community diminishes the total available employment and may also jeopardise the continued employment of many other workers in that community and elsewhere. As the Consett and Port Talbot closures showed in 1980, the repercussions on the lives of the community may be far-reaching. The single number of those made redundant therefore understates the significance for society as a whole.

3.2   YOUTH WITHOUT WORK

Rising unemployment among school leavers and young people in general has attracted increasing concern throughout the 1970s. Successive governments have clearly regarded the young unemployed as deserving the highest priority in man-power programmes, and this was re-emphasised by the November 1980 announcement of an additional quarter of a million pound expenditure on special programmes, which will almost entirely benefit the younger unemployed (see section 4.1). Recognition of the importance of youth unemployment has also been evident in many countries, and international agencies such as OECD and ILO have set up special committees to look into this particular problem. Support for special programmes may be the expression of growing fears about increasing delinquency, hooliganism, crime and general lawlessness when young people with nothing to do become alienated from society and begin to wreak some fearful vengeance upon it or its members. But my experience is that a very large number of people are genuinely concerned about the problems of the young unemployed and feel that this group in particular should not have to bear the burden of increasing unemployment.

The expectations fostered by decades of low unemployment have been frustrated for an ever-increasing number of teenagers. Around 25 per cent of young people under 18 have been registered unemployed at the July counts in recent years, and in July 1980 the rate reached 31 per cent. In July 1981 the prospects are likely to be far worse with unemployment still increasing and a record number of teenagers making their first entry into the labour force. Many school leavers are successful in escaping unemployment within a few months: by November 1980 more than 3 out of 5 school leavers were no longer registering unemployed, and the total had fallen to 111,000, but the number was not far short of *twice* the total at the same time in the previous year. In addition to those still unemployed, some 160,000 young people, including very many who had not worked since leaving school, were enrolled on Youth Opportunities Programmes. While views differ strongly about the extent to which they provide valuable training and work experience, these are not permanent jobs – the majority last about six months (see section 4.1).

The risk of unemployment is very much greater closer to the school leaving age. However, high unemployment among young people is not confined to this group only: 18–19 year olds and 20–24 year olds have the next highest rates of unemployment after those under the age of 18. And these older groups are more vulnerable to prolonged unemployment than any other members of the labour force under the age of 50. Their number out of work over a year rose more than tenfold during the last decade, compared with the doubling among those over 50.

Surveys show a much higher rate of unemployment among young people without any qualifications, and a tendency for this unemployment to be both more frequent and longer lasting. Given this and the fact that the proportion of young people staying on at school rises with social class, it is not surprising that the youngest unemployed come disproportionately from families where the main wage-earner is in manual work, especially unskilled manual work, and therefore also particularly vulnerable to unemployment. One study undertaken for the government in January 1977 found that 1 in 7 young unemployed had fathers out of work, 1 in 5 had a brother or sister unemployed, and the same proportion lived in households where no one was in full-time work. Further evidence of the concentration of unemployment was shown by the fact that nearly 4 out of 5 young unemployed had friends out of work (*Department of Employment Gazette* December 1977, p. 1346). This is one more indication of the way in which unemployment falls much more heavily on certain groups in society.

Evidence that the general rise in unemployment is the basic reason for the particular increase in unemployment among school leavers and young people emerges clearly from a Department of Employment analysis of the various factors leading to youth unemployment. Its conclusion is straightforward and without any qualifications: 'Those conditions which produce high overall unemployment produce high youth unemployment.' Detailed examination of the years 1959–77 shows that, even when school leavers are excluded, young people have been much more prone to unemployment than older workers. When the unemployment rate has gone up by 1 per cent for all males, then the teenage male rate has risen by 1.7 per cent. Teenage girls have been even more vulnerable in a period when female unemployment anyway has climbed faster. For every 1 per cent increase for all women, there has been a rise of 3 per cent among teenagers (*Employment Gazette*, March 1980).

Despite the worsening economic crisis, there are some who still suggest that, after 1981, present forecasts show that the position of young people will improve. The 1970s saw the effect of the rise in the number of births between 1955 and 1965. The declining number of births since 1966 will mean a steady drop of teenagers entering the labour market from 1981 onwards – a decrease as great as there was during the 1960s. But one cannot explain away the current much higher rate of youth unemployment by the increasing number of labour-force entrants alone. It is almost as if the implications of the higher birth rate up to 1965 had been carefully concealed from the nation, as if parents and teachers had engaged in some giant conspiracy to hide the growing number of school children until they were suddenly thrown onto the labour market to swell the dole queue!

In fact, our failure to plan for the increased number of teenage entrants into the labour force, given the considerable visibility of this larger group as they moved into and through their schooling, would astonish many Americans who talk about our planned and 'socialised' economy. By comparison, the United States has had much greater success in accepting a much higher number of teenagers into the labour force. During the 1970s the proportion of the American labour force under the age of 25 increased by more than one-third, but the gap between unemployment rates for youth and the rest of the labour force was actually reduced. In Britain, where the young were not very much more vulnerable to unemployment than others in the early 1970s, the risk of unemployment has become very much greater for young people than for the rest of the labour force (Sorrentino, 1980, p. 176).

Young people have suffered particularly from the general reduction in available jobs. If employers rely on natural wastage with no recruitment to trim their workforce, those coming into the labour force in search of work are particularly vulnerable. Policies of 'last-in, first-out' for redundancies also work against the younger employees. But there have also been changes in the occupational and industrial structure that are exacerbating the problems of young job-seekers. Firstly, many of the jobs such as delivery and messenger boy or domestic servant, traditionally reserved or taken by teenagers, have vanished. Secondly, teenage boys are having increasing difficulty in acquiring a trade – their most common hope and the most general wish of their parents. The long-term decline in apprenticeships has been accelerated by the recession. One consequence is that young people are having to compete for jobs with experienced workers much more than in the recent past. At the same time, equal pay and the need to pay the full adult male rate at 18, or at least earlier than 21, in many jobs have made many young workers more expensive; flat rate incomes policies may have added to this effect. This may partly explain the greater risk of prolonged unemployment among young people over 18. Employers may be much more reluctant to pay them the full adult rate when they can find either older workers with more experience at the same rate or only slightly younger workers at a lower rate.

These developments, combined with a general decline in job opportunities, have meant a downward shift in the career expectations and hopes of many young people. University graduates are now competing with sixth-formers for the jobs that had come to be seen as theirs, while many sixth-formers will be forced into competition with early school leavers. Many employers take advantage of what is happening to recruit 'up market' rather than be forced down to pick up what is left. One recent example is provided by London Transport who advertised in *The Guardian* 'You don't need a University background to drive a bus – but it helps' (23 June 1979): 'It helps a great deal if you are eventually looking for a management career, but feel like a rest from an academic way of life, or are having difficulty in finding a suitable position.' It may also help London Transport who can screen those accepted for subsequent promotion to management, while giving them experience of non-management work at non-management rates.

The result of all these factors is that those already at the end of the queue have the very depressing outlook of seeing the queue growing longer but their position in it remaining the same. With employers using length of time out of work as one means of selection, the newly unemployed appear to have a better chance of acquiring a job than those already out of work, most of whom already seem all too conscious of their deficiencies in the eyes of employers. The deterioration of their chances only appears to magnify their handicaps. Not surprisingly, some who once saw themselves as handicapped now consider they have been disqualified and drop out.

The difficulty of finding work does not lie simply in the lack of jobs; the treatment that young job-seekers often receive in itself is very discouraging. This is reported both by those who have managed to get jobs as well as by those still out of work. An apprentice mechanic wrote:

> What I found really sickening was the attitude of some places you went to look for work they treated you as if you were a nothing and I bet that put a lot of young people off working before they started! [Gow and McPherson, 1980]

But worst of all is the Catch-22 of no-job-without-experience. As one apprentice hairdresser wrote,

> The silly thing about getting a first job is that the interviewer will ask you if you have any experience in that type of job, e.g. hair-dressing – impossible as it is an apprenticeship taken up when left

school. They ask for your name and address, write it down and say they will get in touch when in fact they put it in the bin. [Gow and McPherson, 1980]

The frustration and tensions can be considerable and led one mother to advertise a £50 reward for anyone offering her daughter a job. In 1976, when she could first have left school, her parents persuaded her to go on to the local College of Further Education for two years to gain more qualifications. By then the labour market had deteriorated even further and, with the exception of six months' work experience, 'the next eighteen months were a nightmare of writing after jobs and filling in application forms. We found that some jobs which had only needed 'O' levels wanted 'A' levels now'. She had wanted to be a laboratory assistant but gave this up and took the first job that was offered, working in a small factory. The advertisement brought many offers, mostly 'for hotel staff in the South of England', but they arrived just after she had accepted the job. The pressure on the family has been all the greater because her father had been made redundant twice in the previous twelve months. The real change in the market is emphasised by her mother who pointed out that with higher labour demand in the past it was normal to find better jobs by moving and gaining wider experience (letter from Mrs McArdle, November 1980).

The impact of unemployment comes through vividly and repeatedly in the letters written by young people the year after leaving school in *Tell Them From Me* (Gow and McPherson, 1980). Some say that they would never have left school at the earliest time possible if they had known they would be unemployed for so long, and others are very critical of the school system or the teachers failing to warn and prepare them for the experience of being out of work. Yet others felt rejected already in schools that conspicuously gave more time, concern and energy to educational high-fliers and did little more than attempt to occupy or control those who were taking no examinations.

However, many teachers are well aware of the problems that are going to be facing their students in the coming years. They have no power to create jobs and are conscious of the invidious task of discriminating amongst pupils in references for the very few jobs available. Many discuss it with their classes: 'They could all tell you that there are two million unemployed now, and there are going to be three. And they know they're somewhere in between'. 'We talk about looking for work, going for an interview, where to go and what to say. But it's difficult. You don't want to depress them. You can't take the hope away. You want them to try to find something – it's no good making them too demoralised' (comprehensive teachers in Edinburgh, November 1980).

Essays written by school children in their last term at school in a high unemployment area of the South East in May 1978 revealed a cold awareness of the threat of the dole queue (Pahl, 1978). Similar essays produced by students in their last year at an Edinburgh comprehensive school expressed bleak and often daunting realism. It was perhaps not surprising how many of them expected to escape the dole queue by joining the Forces.

> Many people do not have the chance to get the particular job they would like and just take the first job that comes along and end up unhappy . . . looking for *one* job is hard for me as I do not have any sisters or brothers and my father has a job, but not the kind of job I want – cleaning factory machines and taking orders from other people and having lower wages than a bus driver or something else. Perhaps, after all, I would like a job in the Army where I would enjoy life away from home and out in the fresh air away from the big towns . . . having said all this, I feel that the future leaves much to be desired because I, myself, hoped to join the Army but now I don't [expect to be able to], because more and more people are joining the Forces than ever before because of unemployment which, in turn, demands better education and particular skills.

The lack of resources becomes one factor creating tension and resentment as unemployed young school leavers are unable to keep up with their employed friends or pay their way in 'out of work' activities. The problems of deprivation may be all the greater where there are two family members out of work. Difficulties within their families have emerged in a number of studies and reports from unemployed youths. Even YOP trainees in South London reported that their parents were unsympathetic to their lack of employment

(Into Work South London, Summer report 1980). The tensions were well illustrated in one of the Edinburgh school essays and were also acted out in a drama class at the suggestion of one of the boys who described the difficulties an older brother of his encountered while out of work.

The increasing sense of social rejection felt by young unemployed is mentioned in many studies. The aimless street-corner activity of a group of youths to relieve their boredom can be counter-productive, as Graham Stokes of the University of Birmingham has pointed out.

> A lack of money, a pervasive sense of boredom while in the home and feelings of social isolation lead to meetings in shopping centres, record shops etc. While these are apparently 'innocent', to the passer-by these groups of youngsters would often be perceived as intimidating and suspicious.

This type of activity may be all the more likely to cause problems if the youths are black. The Bullring in Birmingham is a 'magnet' for a number of unemployed black youths, and the management of the Ring are concerned that these groups 'will threaten and deter shoppers and will pilfer from the shops themselves'. Loitering is discouraged by signs and security guards. Youth workers report the uneasy and anxious view that the guards take of black youths, who are likely to get moved on 'if one stops to blow one's nose'. One community worker suggested that 'in usage by Birmingham policemen, the collective noun for a group of 3 or more black youths on the street was a "conspiracy" . . . In the Bullring the young blacks were at least safe from harassment by police if not by security guards' (Allinson and Harrison, 1975, p. 16).

A study of black and white school leavers from Bradford and Sheffield in the early 1970s showed that black youths were much more likely to have difficulty in getting jobs. Although they were no more likely to leave or lose a job once they were in work, they were much more likely to remain longer out of work once they became unemployed (Dex, 1979). The problems and tensions are made all the worse by the way in which some groups are taking advantage of the higher unemployment to whip up racial hatred (see section 5.1).

The school leavers may be the first to be dismissed as part of the 'real' unemployment by some. The Institute of Economic Affairs, for example removes all school leavers, the largest category it extracts from the official figures, in arguing that 'Two million is one million' (Miller, 1980). This is not how they, their parents or their teachers see it as anxieties over future careers increase in the last few terms of school.

While the years of higher employment may have started to equalise chances in the labour force, high unemployment destroys such gains and widens inequalities once again. There is greater pressure on the unqualified to be content with any job, whatever the rewards or quality. Experience of prolonged unemployment or alternating between short-term, dead-end and stultifying jobs clearly diminishes the quality of life for young people, many of whom are denied the chance of a career in any normal sense of the word. With a high level of unemployment there is no encouragement for employers to improve poor-quality and poor-paid jobs since there is a ready pool of unemployed applicants, especially young, who will endure anything for a short period.

3.3 THE DISPOSABLE OLDER WORKER

'Ageism' is still an alien word in English. It has not received the recognition that terms such as sexism and racism have been given, however slow or limited has been the success of tackling problems so deep-rooted in our society. Ageism in terms of discrimination against older workers has been long evident in the unquestioning acceptance of higher and prolonged unemployment. Once older workers lose their jobs, they have very great difficulty in getting back to work, and so form a large proportion of those out of work for many months and years. If their greater vulnerability is noticed at all, it tends to be regarded as natural or inevitable. One comment, for example, made to emphasise the increasing problem of long-term unemployment is that it affects 'not just the older worker'.

In recent years there has been a marked decline in the proportion of men aged 55 and older staying in the labour force, and the drop is even greater for those aged between 60 and 64. Meanwhile there are claims that the older unemployed simply inflate the unemployment figures, stressing the number with occupational pensions (e.g., Miller, 1980). Over half the pensions received by the older men out of work were less than one-quarter of average non-manual earnings at the last survey in 1976 – and less than 1 in 3 men aged 55–64 were known to have an occupational pension at all (*Department of Employment Gazette*, June 1977, p. 574). These facts have received little if any acknowledgement by the deflators of the unemployment statistics, who doubt whether the older unemployed are able or willing to work.

Many others have urged the release of these people from the labour market. Some pensioners' organisations have lobbied for a reduction in the minimum age for claiming the state retirement pension for men, and many unions have negotiated earlier retirement ages in collective bargaining with employers. Emphasis is placed on the demanding and unpleasant form of much work and its harmful, and indeed aging, effect on many workers ('You never see an old welder'). The general focus in talk about retirement on increased leisure and freedom from constraint during the early post-employment days only helps to make such proposals appear more attractive.

Not unnaturally, the enthusiasm for retirement at an earlier age or just at the present minimum has increased with rising unemployment. When the workforce has to be reduced quickly, 'encouragement' to retire earlier is seen as the most suitable measure, very much more acceptable than making workers involuntarily redundant. Early retirement is also the most common and popular solution to youth unemployment: 'They've had their lives: they should move over and let others in' are remarks heard from people of all ages. Many who have retired early themselves endorse the exchange of jobs between old and young: it is 'right to retire if the financial terms are good enough when so many young people are unemployed' (*Employment Gazette*, August 1980, p. 860). Furthermore, earlier retirement enables companies to provide better career prospects for younger staff when the firm is not expanding. Special early retirement provisions in the occupational pension scheme with additional topping-up has, for example, been used by the Midland Bank for this purpose.

It is quite clear that early retirement is acceptable to and even welcomed by many older workers. In one recent survey almost half of the early retired believed that they had 'worked long enough' or 'deserved to retire'. 'Having worked hard, including war service, for nearly 40 years, I thought it was about time my wife and I started to do one or two things that amused us for a change'. Manual workers in particular stressed this factor and many were very conscious of relatives or friends who had died soon after retiring at the normal time. Early retirement, it was believed, would provide a chance to rest and relax and to spend more of their time with their families and with their friends. Many workers had been dissatisfied either with their job in the last few years before retirement or with themselves because they found it 'harder to cope with' their work. 'I was clearly slowing down, my powers of concentration were becoming dulled and a job, which I'd always found so easy, became a burden' (*Employment Gazette*, August 1980, pp. 859–64).

One major consideration, however, has been almost totally ignored, helped by the ways in which we compartmentalise issues. Those concerned with unemployment and those concerned with the needs of older people have both tended to accept the age of retirement as marking the boundary of their field of interest, and there is an increasing tendency to equate 'retired' and 'older' people. In 1921 some 8 out of every 10 men continued working into their late sixties, but today the proportion has fallen below 1 in every 10. The assumption is of a great advance in freeing men from the constraints of work, and the attempts to identify the full extent of labour lost take no account of those past retirement age who would welcome the chance to work, especially in a part-time or flexible arrangement. But what is a divide, a barrier almost, to two separate public policy debates is only a stage in life for the individual. What contribution can earlier retirement make to the problem of unemployment, especially among the young? What is the fairest or the most acceptable way of sharing the declining amount of work available among those who want and need it? And what sort of life should we aim to provide for older people in a society where resources and access to them is very much influenced by the job that they have held? These questions cannot be answered in isolation from each other.

Of course, the current retirement ages of 65 for men and 60 for women are not immutable. The age at which people no longer have to work is not biologically, but socially and politically, determined. One reason for the lowering of the retirement age in 1925 to the present level was the claim that it would release jobs for the younger unemployed. It is a poor reflection on the organisation of our society and a sharp rebuff to beliefs in the general consistency of progress and development in 'modern' or 'advanced' times that we should be moving towards more inflexible and rigid arrangements for retirement for large parts of the population. The only freedom left is to retire earlier. Yet many more people are today fitter and healthier in the second half of their lives than previous generations and more able to continue working. At the same time, the great majority of changes that have occurred in the work process have reduced the proportion of jobs that depend upon brute force and involve great drudgery. The advent of the micro-processor could help to make many jobs lighter and so tenable longer by older people.

Part of the human cost of high unemployment is that the chance of introducing these better opportunities for older workers has now become more remote. The argument that more older people should be allowed to continue to work longer, with much greater flexibility and choice in retirement and less rigid divisions between the worlds of work and non-work has received much less interest in this country than in others. In the United States, for example, one stage in the legal extension of civil rights was the 1968 Age Discrimination in Employment Act. Now this has been amended to protect workers against being forced to retire on the grounds of age alone before the age of 70, and for employees in the Federal Government there is no limit on age grounds at all. This is aimed to 'permit a smoother mix of labour and leisure across life' to bring greater freedom and other benefits to all workers of any age.

There was strong support for the idea of gradual retirement with greater choice and flexibility among early retirees in one recent British survey. But the legislation against discrimination in employment by race and sex, and the efforts of groups initiating and supporting these measures, have had the unintended consequence in Britain of condoning, if not encouraging, discrimination by age. This may have been promoted by policies in the second half of the 1960s. During the 'shake-out' that was supposed to bring 'redeployment', not unemployment, there seemed to be a widespread, and probably growing, acceptance that older workers could and indeed should be laid-off. The operation of the state redundancy schemes encouraged this, whether deliberately or not, by lump-sum payments linked to age and length of service as well as previous earnings.

In contrast to the United States, collective bargaining in Britain has placed little emphasis on the development of seniority arrangements in either promotion or lay-off procedures. Also, the much greater prevalence of apprenticeship schemes for many years provided greater security for young workers in Britain than in the United States. Ironically it was the country that is said to place so much emphasis on youth that gave poorer protection against unemployment to its school leavers and younger workers and greater protection to its older workers. In Britain over the years the opposite applied, until increasing numbers of young people were also forced into the deteriorating labour market.

In the mid-1950s Richard Titmuss forecast the development of 'two nations in old age: greater inequalities in living standards after work than in work' (1958, p. 74). Subsequent research has more than borne out the accuracy of his predictions, showing how these inequalities have their basis in earlier years. 'A major new source of inequality and of poverty in society' is growing from the greater rewards, privileges and benefits gained by many managerial, professional and administrative staff as they move up their occupational hierarchy, while many, particularly among the unskilled and less skilled, are pushed down by the cumulative effect of low pay, increased insecurity, and repeated or prolonged unemployment and often illness (Townsend, 1979, Ch. 19).

> In moving into old age people tend to separate into two groups, one anticipating a comfortable and even earlier retirement, the

other dreading the prospect and depending almost entirely for
their livelihood on the resources made available by the state
through its social security systems. [Townsend, 1979, p. 820]

In total, almost two-thirds of the elderly — some five million
people — existed in or on the margins of poverty (Townsend,
1979, Ch. 23). Since then, the cuts in public expenditure,
with their impact on many of the social services including
housing, are likely to increase the deprivation of many elderly
people.

It is remarkable that these facts have received so little
attention from those arguing for early retirement. One
important element of ageism is the unquestioning acceptance
that the resources of the retired will be less than in work,
although, along with the disabled, they are the group who are
least likely to be able to escape poverty. Recent official
research on the elderly, including early retirement, has failed
to examine the extent of poverty or inequality, while the
DHSS consultative document 'A Happier Old Age' simply
mentions reduced income as something that the old 'must
adjust to'. The acceptance is so great that most old people
themselves are resigned to this fall in their living standards
(for a detailed analysis of these issues, see Walker, forthcoming).

Poverty among the elderly in Britain is greater than in
many other countries because of the inadequacy of our
income maintenance systems for the retired. The real value of
the basic pension has not improved significantly since 1948.
Under the latest pension scheme, 'it will be well into the next
century before most pensioner couples have a pension of half
average earnings' (Piachaud, 1980, p. 178). In retirement, a
minority are supported by generous occupational pensions
and other resources, but those who have experienced previous
unemployment are likely to be amongst the poorest. More-
over, the great majority of those who have retired early will
not be receiving the full pension. Few workers or staff, or
their unions, realise how the operation of many present occupational pension systems tends to penalise the early retired.
With continuing inflation a pension taken early could be half
the value of the full pension in a very short time. This is all
the more disturbing for two reasons. First, a recent govern-

ment study shows how much sickness and ill-health influence the decision to seek or accept early retirement and how frequently these are associated with financial problems. 'This suggests that workers are generally forced into early retirement and not that they opt for it voluntarily' (*Employment Gazette*, April 1980, p. 368). Secondly, the risk of poverty and deprivation increases with the length of time out of work. The economic pressures are much greater therefore on people entering their seventies and eighties than on those who have just retired. Yet these are the people who may need extra resources to spend on transport and a whole range of additional services as they become less mobile and less strong. In addition, many household items such as furnishings, carpets and equipment will need replacement at a time when most capital resources will be exhausted.

The danger for the older worker, unemployed for five or ten years, and for the early retired is that these people will be entering a stage of greater poverty in their sixties rather than later. Besides, both groups are very much less likely to have had the opportunity of carefully replacing and buying in preparation for their retirement. The final twist to this argument is that more and more old people are now living into their seventies and eighties and even beyond. It will become increasingly common for people to spend a quarter or even a third of their lives in retirement. Women are likely to live longer but are generally forced to retire earlier and with a lower pension after a lifetime of lower wages.

For many decades there have been recurrent panics about the 'burden of the aged' because of the expected cost of supporting the economically unproductive years of retirement. The fallacies in this argument have been clearly set out by those who emphasise that we are moving to a more balanced population (e.g. Titmuss, 1958). It is an advance that more people are living longer: the challenge to society is to ensure that this longer life is one that can be enjoyed rather than suffered in increasing poverty. In the last two decades of the twentieth century it seems as if society will actually create this burden of the aged by insisting on more compulsory early retirement while denying adequate resources to the retired to support themselves. At the very time that successive governments strive with increasing fervour to cut public expenditure, their policies are encouraging the creation of dependency on an enormous scale with major short-term and long-term costs. In consequence, it is said that the DHSS is already less in favour of increasing early retirement after calculations of the additional supplementary benefit that would have to be paid out for more years to many more elderly people. Greater demand for health and other social services is also expected, exacerbated by the fact that poverty and bad housing will force many into residential accommodation that imposes further costs on the state.

The concern with increasing expenditure problems should not distract us from recognising the effect on the quality of people's lives. Whether workers leave the labour force after many years of unemployment or are enticed by early retirement provision that in the long-term proves quite inadequate, the effect will be more poverty among old people. In the retirement that society encourages them to anticipate with hope and pleasure, we shall be increasing and prolonging the poverty of the group least able to escape it.

3.4 WOMEN UNEMPLOYED

Many more women are now out of work and their unemployment is lasting longer. In summer 1980 there were twice as many women who had been out of work for the whole of the first six months of the year as were out of work at all ten years ago. The rapid increase in the numbers of women out of work has been one of the most dramatic changes in unemployment during the last decade. From very low levels in the 1950s and 1960s the number of women registered unemployed has increased sevenfold since 1970, compared with a doubling of unemployment amongst men. During the increase in unemployment from 1973 to 1977, registered unemployment amongst women went up twice as fast as for men. During the brief fall after that, male unemployment dropped very much faster than women's.

Part of this increase in the official statistics is the result of legal and administrative changes. The extent of unemployment among women may have become more visible than before. Since April 1978 the reduced National Insurance contribution that married women could opt to pay when they were working has been gradually phased out. Thus, more married women are entitled to unemployment benefit as well as credited contributions maintaining their pension. There is therefore a very much stronger incentive for married women to register when they are out of work, although there are still very many who do not bother. In 1979 almost half the married women and one-quarter of unmarried women who declared themselves as unemployed in the *General Household Survey* interview had not registered at an employment office. Altogether, women made up two-fifths of the unemployed in that survey. There is evidence that the number would have been even larger if child care facilities were better and more widely available. The already very great geographical variations in provision, combined with further cutbacks on expenditure, are liable to widen the differences between areas even more.

One major reason for more unemployment among women has been the fact that over the last thirty years the number of women in the labour force has increased considerably and fairly steadily. The proportion of married women in work has more than doubled, partly replacing the decline in single women resulting from the greater number of marriages. The greatest increase of all has been among women in their midforties and older. In the 1970s alone well over 1 million more women became employed. A very large part of this growth, however, has been in part-time employment with very limited, if any, career prospects, and very often poor rates of pay. Predictions of the increase in working women over the next decade vary greatly, from two-thirds of a million to one and two-thirds million. It has always been notoriously difficult to predict labour force participation among married women. The problem is now even worse because there are factors on both the demand and the supply sides, some of which are encouraging wives to go out to work and others discouraging them. Patterns of work are changing as a result of the changing expectations of women whose years of child-bearing are very much briefer than those of previous generations. In addition, women have been returning to the labour force more speedily than previously. One survey of women who gave birth in early 1979 found that 25 per cent were working and another 15 per cent were looking for jobs within nine months; 2 out of 5 therefore were already back in the labour force (Daniel to House of Lords Select Committee, 1979–1980, vol. ii).

Laws on equal pay and equal opportunities both reflect the changes and encourage them. The pressures of inflation on household incomes further reinforce these changes, which are maintained by the expectations of an adequate, or just higher, standard of living in households with two earners. On the other side, the shifts from manufacturing to service industries, from manual to non-manual jobs, and the increasing willingness to use part-time labour, all serve to create a continuing demand for female labour.

The deteriorating labour market from the middle of the 1970s onward has clearly begun to have a counter-effect: there has been hardly any increase in the proportion of mothers at work since 1975. Redundancies and closures in the textile, clothing and footwear industries, which have always employed a high proportion of women, have been one major cause. Another has been the cutbacks in public expenditure with the subsequent reduction in many full-time and part-time jobs in the whole range of social services in which women have again been heavily concentrated.

The outlook for the future is not at all clear, but there are some ominous signs. Continuing decline in employment in primary industries such as agriculture and mining and in manufacturing will probably generally have less effect on women than men, and those industries that are expected to experience growth include a good proportion where women will benefit. Recent estimates from the Warwick Manpower Research Group (Lindley, 1980) suggest that unemployment amongst men will increase sharply by 1985 with a much smaller rise for women. The continuation of present unemployment trends amongst men means the rate would rise to 18 per cent, with the rate for women climbing to no more than 9 per cent. But, as the Group point out, a major shift in that direction would itself probably provoke major changes. So far, women have had very little success in making inroads into traditional men's jobs, and they have remained disproportionately concentrated in clerical, catering, sales, cleaning and many personal service jobs in addition to the industries, such as textiles, where they have long been established. It seems likely that increasing unemployment amongst men will lead them to encroach on some of the better-paid, more secure and higher-status areas of women's full-time work. At the same time there may be a considerable increase in demands that women, particularly mothers, should stay at home, reinforced by cuts in social services, including child day-care, which enable many to go out to work anyway. There could well be moves against the legislation of the 1970s, which went some way towards establishing 'equal pay for equal work', countering sex-discrimination at work and in hiring and firing, and promoting the rights of mothers to return to their jobs. The swing may go well beyond the limitations to statutory maternity leave already introduced by the present government's amendments of the Employment Protection Act.

By the second half of the eighties the micro-electronic revolution will probably start to have an impact on many areas of female employment, especially in retail sales and some parts of clerical work. Many suggest that the effect of these changes may not only be greater but arrive sooner. Women's opportunities for work could thus be severely cut back under the combined pressure of technological change and men looking for alternative work.

Many people would see this as a desirable development. They regard the *employment* of married women, especially mothers with young children, as the problem, not their *unemployment*. The view that married women should not be in the labour force, taking men's jobs, is indeed a very strong one and has been revived in recent years with rising unemployment. The attack on the creation of 'latchkey' children who wander unprotected into early delinquency is another very powerfully presented argument. The return of mothers to the home to give full-time devotion to their job as the unpaid workers of the community, and not just of their husbands and children, has considerable support. After all, married women's 'failure' to act as unpaid community-carers pushes up public expenditure. When it is examined closely, much of the rhetoric about the virtue and duty of 'community care' can be seen to enshrine long-established traditions about the woman's role (Finch and Groves, 1980). These attitudes are remarkably pervasive throughout British society. They find particularly vigorous expression when new industries move into a depressed area and it becomes evident that these are 'only' bringing jobs for women, which are clearly seen as no adequate replacement for men's jobs. Many wives have stressed to me in interviews that it is not right for a woman to go out to work when her husband is unemployed: 'What man can rest easy when his wife can work and he can not?' 'It's not right to be out at work when your man is not – how will he feel?' These informal pressures seem to be so strong that many women wait until the husband has found work before starting work themselves.

Given the strength of these beliefs at many levels within society, it is perhaps not surprising that we know very much less about the impact of unemployment on women, especially married women. Although the expression itself is outdated, the presumption that married women go out to work for 'pin money' still seems incredibly persistent. The very great effort that women put into managing both their unpaid housework and their paid jobs indicates how important employment is to them. Their extra income may be essential to maintain their own independence and freedom within the marriage and the family. Besides, any household that begins to rely on two adult wage-earners is likely to take on extra commitments to improve the house or its furnishings or equipment, for example. Even the loss of the lower-paid job can create considerable problems, since very many families need two earners just to keep them out of poverty. If the wives were not earning, there would be a 50 per cent increase in the proportion of families in poverty or near poverty even while the husband was in full-time work (Townsend, 1979, p. 631; see also Hamill, 1978). The number of single parents, mainly women, bringing up children by themselves has increased greatly in recent years, and in many of these households the woman's earnings are essential.

One of the proposals put forward to solve the problem of the reduced opportunities for employment, which are expected to decline even faster over the next decade, is the extension of work outside the more formal employment structure and in the home. Yet among women, who already have generally poor employment opportunities and rewards, homeworkers 'are probably the most heavily exploited and underprivileged workers in the country' and in recent years their number has tended to increase (TUC, 1980?). They include some of the most marginal members of the labour force — if they can even be described as that — many of them women with family commitments to look after young children and elderly or disabled relatives that prevent them from leaving home. Others are disabled or retired with restricted mobility, and a third, particularly vulnerable group are immigrants (Low Pay Unit, 1980). These workers tend to survive in poverty in and out of work very little protected by laws. The danger of increasing unemployment and poverty among women is that those who are already most vulnerable, yet least visible, will be forced to undertake this form of home-working. Whether working or unemployed, they rarely appear in any official statistics of the labour force.

Despite the increase, and growing visibility, of unemployment among women, we still know very much less about the full extent of their problems in the labour market and its impact upon them and their families. Some of the attacks on the official unemployment figures for overcounting leave the impression that many, if not most, of the unemployed can be classified in two ways — those who won't work and those who shouldn't be in the labour force anyway. Among the second group are not only the occupational pensioners and other older unemployed who should be treated as early retired, but married women. 'Married women taking men's jobs' is a common reason put forward to explain part of the increase in overall unemployment, and is one I have heard frequently in traditional working-class areas.

Detailed comparative evidence, however, shows that, first, unemployment among women in Britain is not greater than among men, even allowing for the unregistered unemployed. This is in sharp contrast to most other industrial countries where female unemployment is very much higher. Second, a far greater proportion of married women has been entering the labour force in other countries than in Britain, yet there has not necessarily been any accompanying rise in overall levels of unemployment (Sorrentino, 1980). There is clearly a need to examine the problems of women out of work much more closely. The disregard or neglect of their unemployment is further evidence that Britain still does not view married women in particular as full members of the labour force.

3.5 THE LONG-TERM UNEMPLOYED

> Prolonged unemployment is for most people a profoundly corrosive experience, undermining personality and atrophying work capacities. And it is an experience to which some of the worst disadvantaged groups in our society . . . are particularly vulnerable, and all are more vulnerable in areas of high unemployment.
> [Harrison, 1976, p.347]

This forthright and unequivocal paragraph is the conclusion to a review of research on effects of long-term unemployment published in the official *Department of Employment Gazette* during the last sharp rise in unemployment. Subsequent research has only supported this conclusion. Since then, developments in the economy and the labour market have resulted in an increasing number of people being out of work for longer periods. In October 1980 over 730,000 men and women had been registered as unemployed for six months or more, and over 400,000 for a year or longer. Over the last decade long-term unemployment has grown even faster for women than for men, reflecting their higher increase in unemployment generally. However, women are less likely to remain on the register and so the evidence for men is a more reliable indication of the full extent of prolonged unemployment. In October 1980 nearly 2 out of every 3 men registered unemployed had been out of work for six months or more, and over 1 in 5 more than a year. More than 1 in 13 had been registered unemployed for at least 3 years — 106,000 men.

During 1980 the total unemployed rose sharply and vacancies plummeted. While some of the longer unemployed will have retired and others fallen sick, very few will have been successful in returning to work. It is generally expected that the total out of work for over a year in 1981 will rise towards three-quarters of a million, and that the number unemployed for six months will go past the million mark — fifteen years after *total* unemployment first climbed to 600,000 after the war. The virtual doubling of the numbers out of work within the year caused an uproar at the time.

The increase in the long-term unemployed is all the more important because prolonged unemployment has been a more persistent problem in Britain than in many other countries. Even during the years of low unemployment we had a particularly high proportion of long-term unemployed. In the mid-1960s the rate of long-term unemployment in Britain appeared almost as high as that of Canada and the United States where overall levels of unemployment were much higher. Over the last couple of years the United States and the United Kingdom have had fairly similar rates of unemployment (after adjustment for differences in the definition and collection of statistics), but the proportion of unemployed with more than six months out of work has been dramatically higher in the United Kingdom (one-third or more, compared with one-ninth or less in the United States). While these figures are not collected on the same basis, it is extremely unlikely that the statistical differences could account for this gap.

Some people, predominantly on the political right, have claimed that many of the long-term unemployed should be omitted from the count because they are not really employable. It may seem eminently reasonable to exclude from the 'real' count those who declare that they are not looking for work and are only registering because it is a condition of their receiving benefit and credited National Insurance contributions, so that it is the system of administering benefits that forces them to be classified as unemployed. The great weakness in this argument is that it ignores the actual impact of increased unemployment on those out of work. By removing the long-term unemployed, we actually conceal the significance of increased unemployment for some of those worst affected.

The lack of success in finding work has an effect on the intensity with which the unemployed continue to search for work. One worker who had been fourteen months out of work in mid-1979 reflected, 'six months ago I was despondent, but now I'm getting accustomed to it . . . I don't think I'm actually the less employable . . . I'm still trying'. Another long-term unemployed said, 'Before, I used to sit and glare at the paper, or walk round and ask people. Now I just take it as it comes', though he still phones up for jobs he sees advertised. They were both adjusting to the problems of prolonged unemployment. 'It does bother me. But if you ponder on it, you'd go loony' (Colledge and Bartholomew, 1980, Ch. 5). The need to adapt in order to survive psychologically was emphasised by this official report, by the Manpower Services Commission, from which these quotations have been taken.

> There comes a point [when] people can no longer sustain their motivation in the face of continued rejection, heightened awareness of their own shortcomings, disillusion with job finding services, belief that all available options have been covered, and a knowledge that jobs are scarce anyway. [Colledge and Bartholomew, 1980, 5.4]

The collapse of confidence in their ability to carry out even their old trade, let alone a new job, is a common theme. Another tradesman in his early thirties and out of work for a year commented:

> I have lost a lot of confidence in myself, I have particularly lost confidence that I can do new jobs, and I am also nervous about getting back to do work within my own trade. Before I would have tried anything . . . you see a year ago I would have had a go. But it is difficult to say how I feel, its a funny feeling. I'm worried about not having a job but at the same time I'm worried that I won't be able to do the job when I get it . . . but I am trying. Sometimes after I have been turned down for another job, I begin to think there is something wrong with me. Talking now, I know there aren't any jobs and it is not me at fault. But after you have been for a few interviews you get depressed and start to lose your confidence.

He had been particularly depressed during the bad weather of last winter: 'I was stuck indoors all the time. I would try and think of anything to try and pass the time, but more often than not I would just sit there staring at the wall. The frustration is really bad. You want to do something but you can't.' (Newcastle, 1980, pp. 36–7). The very decline in confidence that results from months and years out of work saps the energy and determination to keep looking for work. This may help to reinforce a downward spiral or 'a vicious circle in the relationship between the unemployed and the rest of the community which may make it even more difficult for people who have been out of work for a long time to get back into full-time employment' (Newcastle, 1980, p. 39). It may also be seen as unwillingness to work, supporting assumptions of a carefree, taxpayer-supported life of luxury on the 'Costa del Dole'.

Yet the evidence of many surveys shows that the long-term unemployed are generally among the very poorest in Britain today. Indeed, many contend that the increasing poverty of prolonged unemployment itself contributes to the demoralisation that weakens the determination to push for work. Those long out of work tend to withdraw from society and to expect less so that their poverty and distress become less visible. The full extent of deprivation from prolonged unemployment may only become evident after a number of meetings with a family, and among the long-term unemployed those with children to support are particularly liable to be poor (see section 2.4). As already emphasised, the risk of poverty is all the greater in families where the main wage-earner is unskilled, because those without skills are particularly vulnerable to prolonged unemployment, and their resources are often already reduced through previous unemployment or sickness or poor wages in their last job.

Of course, prolonged unemployment is not a uniform experience. People becoming unemployed do not start off equal. Previous earnings, current savings and access to financial and other help, the security of past employment and the level of demand for one's skills, if any, all affect the impact of a spell out of work. Declining resources weigh even more heavily as unemployment stretches on, and even the most optimistic become despondent.

> Apart from the frustration and boredom there is the worry. There is the heating and other bills, the future, the uncertainty, the wondering – things always on your mind. You can't stop thinking about them. The worry is always there – day and night, I can't sleep at night for worrying. . . . I am much more bad tempered than I used to be, I jump on things much quicker now. I have

changed a lot in myself. I think not having money is a bad thing.
[Newcastle, 1980, pp. 37–8]

Recognising that their length of unemployment, age, poor
health, disability, lack of skill or obsolescent skill put them
at the back of the queue in terms of employers' preference,
many long-term unemployed in particular are likely to become
resigned to the remote chance of finding work in competition
with the younger, more able and more skilled. But this does
not mean that they could not or would not work if jobs were
available. Those who had experience of recruiting scarce
labour during the last war produce quite remarkable accounts
of men or women whose very long unemployment did not
prevent them from successfully taking up work again. A
colleague recalls a woman with a length of unemployment
and work record that would discourage the most optimistic
employer, yet who turned out to be a highly competent
crane driver. Statistical evidence indicates that such recollections are not just the vivid and eccentric exceptions. During
the depression the Unemployment Assistance Board vigorously
stressed that the failure to look for work reflected the 'apathy
and listlessness . . . bred by long periods of unemployment'.
Its wartime successor, the Assistance Board, reinforced this
point by emphasising the dramatically reduced number of
unemployed recipients in 1944 (Leicester 6, Birmingham 8,
Bristol 30, the whole of the London Civil Defence Region
500, and none at all in Rugby and Reading – Deacon, 1980b).
War cannot be a policy option in the battle against long-term
unemployment, but we must recognise that 'unemployability'
is a function of the level of demand for labour and that it is
the situation, not the people who are classified as unemployable, that is the basic cause of prolonged unemployment.

Many more people can be absorbed into the labour force if
the work is available and this has been shown during peace
time. One may compare the 401,000 people who have been
registered as unemployed for a whole year at least with the
equivalent figure of some 20,000 for mid-1956 when very
long-term unemployment was at its lowest since the war, and
the general concern was with overfull employment. The
twentyfold increase over the twenty-four years is a vivid illus-

tration of the deterioration of the labour market for those who are most likely to have the greatest difficulty in finding work.

More important than whether or not those suffering prolonged unemployment are unemployable is whether they will ever have the chance to work again and the impact of this on them and their families. Yet the scale of this problem is disguised by current official evidence and debate. The official statistics only tell us how long somebody has been registered as unemployed in one uninterrupted period. If a person becomes ill and claims sickness benefit for more than a few days, he will be taken off the unemployment register. If he becomes unemployed again after that, his official duration of unemployment will commence again at the date he re-registers. Daniel has calculated that the 'true' figure of unemployed out of work for more than a year was 500,000 when the Department of Employment Statistics set it at just over 300,000 (House of Lords Select Committee, 1980, vol. ii, p. 19). In early 1980, therefore, it is likely that 40 per cent had been out of work for more than a year when the official figures showed 25 per cent *registered* unemployed for that long.

More seriously, the Department of Employment and other official agencies have helped to conceal the extent and problem of long-term unemployment by slipping into accepting one year out of work as the measure. Twenty or even ten years ago the cut-off point of six months appeared to be more generally accepted. Certainly it was the duration I was encouraged to use by British officials as well as others when carrying out a review of evidence on the long-term unemployed in ten OECD member countries in the mid-1960s (Sinfield, 1968). Evidence on the experience of unemployment indicates that six months is more appropriate. Such a length of time out of work can no longer be described as seasonal or due to particularly bad weather conditions. It also approximates to the time when many unemployed drop to a lower level of benefit with the exhaustion of the earnings-related supplement (see section 4.2). Although that is to be abolished by April 1982, six months is still a better guide to when resources start to get tight, even for those with previously high earnings and redundancy payments to cushion the initial blow.

This may seem a trivial point but it shows how, consciously and unconsciously, we can act to redefine and so diminish the apparent scale of a problem as it becomes more intractable. Being out of work for many months and years may seem a severe enough problem by itself. It might be thought that for this reason alone there would be particular sympathy from the rest of the community for those people who are unfortunate enough to remain out of work a long time, and special measures to help them. The fact is that the long-term unemployed tend to be treated as second-class citizens. Over the years there has been mounting evidence of the ways in which they still remain at best neglected and more commonly discriminated against and rejected.

It is possible that greater sympathy will emerge because the sharp increase in unemployment makes the rest of the community much more aware that there are fewer jobs and there will be greater tolerance of those who remain at the back of the queue. But my own expectation in the past of more sympathetic attitudes during increased unemployment makes me much less optimistic. In 1975 and 1976, for example, unemployment rose by 75 per cent within the two years. But this period witnessed the harshest outcry against the unemployed since the war, and it was evident that many people believed that the longer someone was out of work, the more likely they were to be fiddling, scrounging or just idling. Some exception was made for the older unemployed, but even willingness to recognise their plight was not accompanied by any support for more generous treatment (Deacon, 1978).

Past experience also indicates that hostility towards the long-term unemployed may grow as soon as the total level of unemployment drops. In 1964 for example, after the very sharp shock of the recession of the winter of 1962/3, I found considerable suspicion and resentment towards those who had not returned to work. One town clerk in the north-east of England told me that 'only the dregs were left on the dole'. In a society where there continues to be much distrust and suspicion of anyone not working, length of time out of work becomes a crude indicator to the rest of us of how hard somebody is trying to find work, especially when there is evidence of some jobs available and some people returning to work.

Employers' recruitment practices tend to operate against the long-term unemployed because the length of time since the candidate last worked is often used as a means of selecting from a pool of applicants. Some employers may simply consider that workers deteriorate as their time out of work lengthens and prefer someone who has evidently been fit enough to hold down a job more recently. Others believe the length of unemployment indicates lack of industry and a willingness to work. Either way, the unemployed may find it more difficult to obtain jobs the longer they are out of work — one more Catch 22 that faces those worst affected by unemployment. The greater the pool of unemployed the more such a criterion works against those longer out of work, and the shorter the time limit imposed by employers.

A few employers are not so choosy, however, offering mindless, unpleasant and dully repetitive work that is likely to drive most recruits away fairly quickly. And it is in these jobs that many of those who have had most difficulty in finding work may eventually finish up, especially perhaps those who are encouraged, cajoled or simply frightened into work by Unemployment Review Officers (see section 4.2).

If it is only natural, as most people seem to think, that those first out of work are likely to be amongst the last to find a new job when unemployment falls, it seems equally self-evident that we should do all we can to ensure that those who bear the longest burden of unemployment should not be diminished by the experience. And if, as many argue, 2 million out of work is going to be seen as the norm, or even the lowest that can be managed in our changing economy, then the need to support the long-term unemployed is made even greater.

CHAPTER FOUR

Services for the Unemployed

4.1 THE EMPLOYMENT SERVICE AFTER THE CUTS

The main services for the unemployed are provided through
the employment service and the social security system. The
employment service is now a division of the Manpower Services
Commission which was set up with considerable initiative and
promise by the Conservative government in 1973 and developed with some vigour and enthusiasm by the subsequent
Labour government. In seven years it has achieved more than
many longer-established departments. On the issue of unemployment it has publicly criticised successive governments,
but it is doubtful whether a more cautious and deferential
attitude would have prevented the massive cuts made by a
government elected on a manifesto to reduce government
intervention. Any government that intends or just allows
'industrial discipline' to be maintained or re-established by
rising unemployment is bound to see particular value in
cutting labour market policies. In addition, some Conservative ministers and MPs are said to regard the MSC as too
powerful, and others have criticised it for supporting such
organisations as the Newcastle Centre for the Unemployed.

The political and financial emasculation of the Manpower
Services Commission is likely to be regarded by historians as
one of this government's most short-sighted acts. This has
particularly disturbing implications for the long-term development of the economy, for Britain was slow to move into the
era of active manpower policies inaugurated by Sweden and
other countries and vigorously promoted by OECD some
fifteen years ago. The development of the British manpower

services has been well documented by Brian Showler (1976) up to the mid-1970s and by Michael Hill (1980a,b) over the last decade. The ways in which long-term goals became swiftly overtaken by more immediate and short-term political concerns emerges clearly in their accounts.

The work of the Commission covers three areas: employment services, training services and special programmes. The establishment of an effective employment service and the development of a very much more up-to-date training system are both vital to Britain's economic recovery. Given the impending scale of technological change predicted by even the most conservative of analysts, Britain's ability to train and retrain to take advantage of the new technological processes might seem to be essential to any government in power, whatever its ideology. Yet the latest announcements, on top of the previous slide towards emergency and palliative measures, mean that by 1981 the MSC will be spending some 43 per cent of its budget on special programmes. Only five years earlier the special programmes took up under 8 per cent of the total budget, allowing a greater proportion of energy, time and resources to be devoted to the long-term improvement of employment and training services.

Some of the early MSC measures were admittedly naive and crude, but the whole effort of the Commission became diverted, if not subverted, towards the camouflage of rising unemployment under successive Labour administrations. The 'body-count' mentality of temporary measures to absorb as many unemployed as possible resulted in an alphabet soup of programmes over the second half of the 1970s:

Temporary Employment Subsidy (TES) – Temporary Short-Time Working Compensation Scheme (TSTWCS) – Small Firms' Employment Subsidy (SFES) – Recruitment Subsidy for School Leavers (RSSL) – Youth Employment Subsidy (YES) – Adult Employment Subsidy (AES) – Job Creation Programme (JCP) – Special Temporary Employment Programme (STEP) – Work Experience Programme (WEP) – Community Industry (CI) – TSA courses for young people (TSAYP) – Youth Opportunities Programme (YOP) – Training places in Industry (TI) – Job Introduction Scheme for disabled (JIS) – Job Release Scheme (JRS) [Lindley, 1980, p.345]

As understanding of manpower problems has developed with increasing experience, the Commission has become better placed to mount a major series of policy initiatives. But not only has its budget been severely cut, the problems it has to tackle have grown dramatically with the 60 per cent rise in registered unemployment over the last twelve months, so that strategies for active manpower policy that would help to build and maintain full employment or much lower unemployment have not been allowed to develop. Programmes integrated with the work of bodies such as the Equal Opportunities Commission and the Race Relations Board to promote more equal employment opportunities for groups that suffer some form of disadvantage or discrimination have never really surfaced. Given the persisting significance of the employment structure for maintaining and legitimating major social and economic inequalities in our class-bound society, it is essential to develop policies to contribute to an attack upon these inequalities. Like other government departments, the MSC has been required to cut its expenditure and the number of its employees. The scale of the staff cuts will bring reductions of 30 per cent by April 1984 in comparison with the planned increase under the last administration. The cuts so far have meant a reduction of 13 per cent but this, it should be stressed, is without allowing for the fact that the main customers of the MSC have risen by three-fifths in one year. The result of these cuts and ministerial pressures has meant increasing emphasis on programmes for school leavers and young people with explicit or concealed cuts in services for other groups including the disabled and the adult long-term unemployed.

The major initiatives in the first programmes were Job Creation (JCP) and Work Experience (WEP). The adverse reaction provoked by some of the early efforts, such as counting lampposts in streets, obscured some of the more lively and thoughtful projects that provided a valuable range of services within the community – for example, the Ironbridge Museum in Coalbrookdale. This provision of 'short term jobs of social value' was dropped because of the impossible constraints: 'Jobs had to be worthwhile to the workers and to the community, but also temporary and not substitutes for jobs that would otherwise have been done' (M.J. Hill,

1980a, p.208). But JCP was used to support 'relatively low priority local authority jobs at a time when authorities are having to cancel or defer more important work because of public expenditure constraints' (MSC, 1977, quoted in Hill, 1980a).

Of the main special programmes now surviving, the largest is the Youth Opportunities programme (YOP), which provides preparation for work and experience in work for school leavers and others up to 18. The payment of wages in the abandoned Job Creation programme has been replaced by a weekly tax-free allowance, now at £23.50. In November 1980 the Secretary of State for Employment undertook to provide 440,000 YOP places for 1981/2 which means an increase of 180,000 on 1980. At present, some 65 per cent of pupils leave school in England and Wales at the age of 16 and 'most of that group have no, or relatively modest, formal education' in the view of the MSC. The object of the new measures is to provide a chance for all unemployed school leavers to enter a YOP scheme by the following Christmas instead of the following Easter as at present (and within three months to any 16 or 17 year old who has been unemployed for three months, instead of twelve months as at present). There should also be more opportunity for the one-third of YOP members who do not have a job at the end to continue into another scheme – and of course the proportion tends to be greater in areas hardest hit by unemployment. The particular advantage of the change is that many school leavers have had to wait as long as a year before joining any scheme, however limited.

In recent years, 1 in 5 of the YOP participants have been on work preparation courses, generally about three months long. The rest have been on work experience programmes on employer's premises, usually lasting for six months. 'We are trying, as resources permit, to work towards the point where every 16 and 17 year old not in education or a job will be assured of vocational preparation lasting as necessary up to his or her 18th birthday' (Mr Prior, 21 November 1980). The Secretary of State hailed this 'extremely ambitious programme' as 'nothing less than a *new deal* for the young unemployed'. Yet he simply seems to have restored YOP to the level it might already have reached if the more expansionary plans of the Labour government had not been cut so severely. Cynics with a clear memory of lower unemployment are tempted to see the Tory 'new deal' in the declining opportunities for training and the sharp rise in unemployment, trapping school leavers in the Catch 22 of no work without experience and no experience without work.

The second main measure has been the Special Temporary Employment Programme (STEP). Largely replacing the Job Creation programme, the jobs are temporary, usually for a year, and publicly funded at the 'appropriate negotiated rate'. Its entrants have been equally divided between the unemployed aged 19–24 and 25 and over. For the younger group, priority is given to those with six months unemployment, and for the older to those with over twelve months. The scheme, however, has suffered severely in the cuts. In 1977 the MSC planned some 25,000 temporary jobs a year throughout the country with a bias towards areas of higher unemployment. The Conservative government cut it back by half and limited it to depressed areas and certain inner-city districts. STEP is now to be replaced by the Community Enterprise Programme (CEP) in April 1981. This will aim to provide 25,000 filled places by March 1982, way behind the target under the previous plan.

The reality of this 'massive practical demonstration of our concern for the unemployed', as the Secretary of State for Employment described it, is highly debatable. Unless there has been a major and effective change in government policy, the number of people registered unemployed for over six months will have exceeded 1 million by spring 1982 and the number over a year some three-quarters of a million. Despite CEP, there is a further shift towards help for the young unemployed. Their needs are important but so are those of the other and longer unemployed.

Another measure that survives is the Job Release Scheme. In February 1980 this was restricted by lifting the age of eligibility for men from 62 to 64 although disabled *men* could leave their jobs from the age of 60. In November it was announced that this would continue for at least one more year for these groups as well as for women aged 59. Already the programme has apparently taken some 100,000 people off the register (*Hansard,* 26 November 1980, col. 673).

Finally, the November package included an extension of the Temporary Short-Time Working Compensation Scheme (TSTWCS). This was introduced in April 1979 for employers who agreed to withdraw an impending redundancy of ten or more workers. Employers were refunded 75 per cent of normal wages paid to the staff working short time to avoid redundancy plus the cost of the National Insurance contributions for the workless days. The scheme has been extended from six months to nine months although the refund is now limited to 50 per cent. This has been used almost exclusively by the manufacturing firms, particularly in engineering, textiles, clothing and footwear, and more generally in high unemployment areas. One survey in mid-1979 showed that about a third of firms using TSTWCS had declared a redundancy in the last year and about 1 in 10 had made more than 20 per cent of their labour force redundant during that period (*Employment Gazette,* May 1980). At that date at least a quarter of the firms believed that the scheme had helped them to avoid redundancies. With the dramatic increase in liquidations and redundancies over the last year, the protection that can be provided by this scheme is likely to be very much more limited. For firms that can survive, however, the scheme may help them to retain their skilled labour force.

In addition to these schemes, there has been much discussion of and some experiment with subsidies to employers for recruiting members of certain groups. There is already a dilemma that highly visible special programmes for particular groups, such as the young or the disabled, may help to reinforce existing prejudices. Work preparation courses, subsidies, exemptions from employers' National Insurance contributions and so on may be aimed to 'improve the "marketability" of those against whom the labour market discriminates'. But this may do much more to foster 'the belief that our problems lie with the supply of, rather than the demand for, labour, and thus reinforce the tendency to "blame the victim" for his own unemployment' (M.J. Hill, 1980b).

There may well be a limit to the number of special groups that can be given any real priority by a variety of different schemes and 'wheezes' (as a Department of Employment senior civil servant described them to the House of Lords Select Committee on Unemployment). The number and variety of different measures for young people in the mid-1970s alone created considerable confusion among employers and began to appear counter-productive. But, in concentrating on the young unemployed, there has been increasing neglect and disregard of other groups who are vulnerable or seen as marginal in the labour force, including the disabled, the older worker and the long-term unemployed. The Department of Employment and the Manpower Services Commission have both collected very clear evidence of the hardships of the long-term unemployed and could have done very much more to support the case of the Supplementary Benefits Commission and the DHSS Supplementary Benefits Review team in arguing that the long-term social security rates should be made available to the long-term unemployed.

The case for this equal treatment in the social security system is all the greater given that the MSC's own studies have demonstrated its failure or inability to offer significant help to the long-term unemployed. Three-quarters of those out of work for more than two years and two-thirds of those unemployed between one and two years have *never* been submitted for a job by the state employment service. Some have argued that discrimination against the longer unemployed has increased with the 'modernisation' of the employment service since the early 1970s (Layard, 1979), because they have less contact with the placing staff in the job centre.

But marked deterioration in employment service help for the long-term unemployed is probably less significant than the continuing neglect of this group. In 1965 the Permanent Secretary to the Ministry of Labour told an OECD conference that 'the duty of the service will always be first to those who are least able to help themselves'. But evidence of any sustained implementation of this duty has never been made available. The Special Employment Needs (SEN) scheme was an important initiative to give more help in obtaining work for the hard-to-place and had shown some results. It is estimated that some three times as many long-term unemployed left the register with help from this special planning scheme than would have left through employment offices. But each successful placing in this scheme cost three and a half times more than the average in the general service, and, with the requirement to make cuts, the employment service took the decision that it could not afford the extra costs of the experimental scheme. It was axed before they had even completed the pilot project for it.

It has, of course, to be a matter of judgement whether this expensive work is sufficiently valuable. Should special priority be given to the hard-to-place with some resultant cut in ordinary placing work? This is a harsh dilemma for a service that is still trying to shake off the image of the dole queue and to obtain notification of a greater proportion of all the jobs available. There is a real danger that such a strategy would result in employers not bothering to contact job centres, from which the long-term unemployed might lose even more.

Nevertheless, the failure to develop any programme to help the long-term unemployed is a major deficiency for the group that is probably in greatest need in the labour market. The new CEP, which replaces STEP, will provide a few thousand places for the very long-term unemployed over 25, but this is an insignificant contribution towards helping the fast increasing number of those long out of work. One particular irony of this failure to increase programmes such as these is that their expansion 'creates employment of a kind least likely to cause inflationary pressure, is more easily contracted and is much less expensive in terms of its implications' for the public sector borrowing requirement (Lindley, 1980, p.357).

Meanwhile the only special scheme that remains available to these unemployed seems to be the work of the Unemployment Review Officers (UROs) of the Department of Health and Social Security. They are expected to keep all unemployed recipients of supplementary benefit 'under review' and to discuss their efforts to find work with them (Hill, 1980b, pp.111–13). Instead of a careful integration of the employment and income services to help the long-term unemployed and hard-to-place, the only programme is one strongly associated with measures to check fraud and abuse (see the next section).

Evidence from studies in Britain as well as other countries

shows that the most effective way of helping those who are most likely to become long-term unemployed is to give them particular help as soon as they become unemployed. It is even better to help to reduce their chances of becoming unemployed in the first place by adjusting redundancy compensation and other measures. Once people are unemployed, it is very much more difficult to find work again. The vivid conclusion of the Pilgrim Trust study in 1938 is still very apt: those out of work 'are not simply units of employability who can, through the medium of the dole, be put in cold storage and taken out again immediately they are needed. While they are in cold storage, things are likely to happen to them' (p.67).

No effective substitute for an adequate demand for labour has been devised to bring those who are hard to employ — or have become regarded so — back to work on any significant scale. The most detailed and comprehensive study based on comparative evidence concluded that 'the maintenance of overall unemployment rates at 2% or less for years at a time may be the single most important factor in minimising the number of hard to employ and motivating a programme to seek the residual group who might appear unemployable . . . at 4% unemployment' (Reubens, 1980, p.384). Without much lower unemployment even the most active manpower policies cannot make any long-term contribution unless they are dramatically expanded rather than cut back. To provide programmes on the scale available in Sweden would have demanded at least a fourfold increase in the proportion of gross national product devoted to these measures even before the cuts made by the Conservatives.

Nevertheless, to direct so much of the remaining resources toward one deserving group to the exclusion of others whose needs also merit recognition is to leave these even more vulnerable and deprived. Much more needs to be done in making government and the wider public aware of the difficulties of these neglected groups, especially those whose problems are compounded by the concentration of effort on others. In examining the workings of the different parts of the social security system in the next section, it is all the more important to investigate the extent to which the more disadvantaged position of groups such as the long-term unemployed is recognised and compensated for.

4.2   SOCIAL SECURITY AND ECONOMIC INSECURITY

The most controversial of all government activities in relation to the unemployed are the income maintenance schemes. This has always been so, and the most persistent question has been about the effect that income support out of work has on the incentive to work. Concern is not confined to the motivation of the unemployed alone. If benefits are too generous, it is feared that workers will give up their jobs when it suits them and will generally be less responsible. Unemployment will no longer be able to serve what many still see as its primary function – the preservation of the authority of employer over worker. Others attack the inadequacy of income support and stress the effect of deprivation and poverty on the unemployed and their families, and the extent to which the problems of the loss of work are compounded by loss of income. They also fear that the unemployed may be insufficiently protected from employers who pay inadequate wages for poor jobs, thus reinforcing the link between low pay and poverty in and out of work.

The discussion about benefits is therefore not a narrow technical issue. It touches on central beliefs about the proper relationship between worker and employer and the role of the state in intervening between them, about what motivates people to work and what sort of society we wish to live in. This debate has a very long history. A visiting European sociologist reflected that the British have been obsessed with the problem of work incentives since the earliest poor laws in 1349. An American analyst has also argued that the fear of 'able-bodied' people settling down on state benefits has been the most persistent political concern in social policy for some six centuries (Mencher, 1968).

The two main benefits received by the unemployed are National Insurance unemployment benefit and supplementary benefits. There are other benefits, allowances or payments (or exemptions from payments for services) that the unemployed may obtain, but insurance benefit is the only one that is directed specifically towards the unemployed; supplementary benefit is the main provision for those without adequate resources and not working. Redundancy payments, it should be remembered, are compensation for loss of a job, not unemployment, and under the state scheme are paid whether the ex-worker goes straight into another job or remains unemployed. Many people on insurance benefit receive either a rent or rate rebate or both. But these do not go to anyone on supplementary benefit, whose rent and rates are paid.

The basic *insurance benefit* is paid for up to one year to unemployed who have established that they are usually regular members of the labour force by making the required amount of National Insurance contributions. The present weekly benefit is £20.65 with additional payments of £12.75 for an adult dependant and £1.25 for each child. No benefit is paid for the first four days out of work. After two weeks an *earnings-related supplement* is paid for six months to registered unemployed over 18 who qualify for the basic or flat-rate benefit. The maximum addition is just under £18 a week. The present government, however, has already begun important changes that are substantially reducing the extent of support to the unemployed at a time when unemployment is now the main cause of increasing poverty. In November 1980, the purchasing power of the flat-rate benefit was increased by 5 per cent *less* than the rise in prices. Combined with changes in the addition for children and Child Benefit, this means an additional loss to unemployed families with children of nearly £3 a week. Furthermore, the earnings-related supplement will be abolished in April 1982 and the maximum has already been cut to £14 in January 1981. The total effect of these various cuts will force far more people to apply for the means-tested benefits. The Supplementary Benefits Commission itself has estimated that these changes may result in the number of unemployed claimants of supplementary benefit rising to 1½ million in two years – a trebling on the May 1980 figures.

The basic problem in the insurance system is a simple but long-standing one. Intended as 'social security' for the unemployed, it has collapsed, and its deficiencies have become more glaring as the numbers out of work, especially the long-term unemployed, have risen. Only 45 per cent of those registered as unemployed at the special annual analysis in May 1980 were receiving insurance benefit. It is eight years since the proportion of men receiving insurance benefit was even as high as one-half (unpublished data supplied by the DHSS).

There are two main reasons why somebody can be registered unemployed but not be entitled to insurance benefit. The first is that they have failed to earn their entitlement with enough contributions before they become unemployed. This particularly affects young people coming straight from school or after only a short period of employment. For them this must seem an additional twist to their Catch 22: they cannot get a job because they have not had work experience and vice versa − but they cannot get any compensation for being unemployed because they have not had a job where they could make their contributions. Women who have been out of the labour force for a while, giving birth to or bringing up children, may also fail to qualify when they register for work. Many other married women are ineligible because they have not paid the full insurance contribution while employed (see section 3.4). In recent years the contribution conditions have changed from requiring a set number of weeks' contributions to allowing a person to qualify when they have paid contributions on so many times the weekly lower earnings limit. This obviously enables the higher paid worker to qualify for benefit somewhat faster than the lower paid. This of course is all the more likely to work against women whose earnings on average are still substantially below the earnings of men despite the Equal Pay Act.

The second main reason for not receiving insurance benefit may seem even more bizarre. It is not that the unemployed have not worked enough before becoming unemployed but that they have been unemployed for too long. The benefit is not paid after 312 days − that is, twelve months on a six-day week basis. Over the last ten years the proportion of men out of work at the May count who have used up or 'exhausted' all their benefit has ranged from nearly 1 in 4 to more than 1 in 3. As more and more people join the swelling total unemployed for a year or longer − likely to reach three-quarters of a million by the end of 1981 — the numbers deprived of insurance benefit grow. Nearly 300,000 men had exhausted their full benefit by May 1980, and this total will rise sharply as many more are forced to remain longer out of work. If these people were ill, we would treat them very differently. After six months of earnings-related supplement, they would qualify for invalidity pension at a higher rate than the basic insurance benefit. This would continue as long as they were incapable of work until they reached retirement age. A couple with two children would receive £56.60, compared with £35.90 paid to the unemployed (and then only for a total of twelve months). The invalidity benefit, more than half as much again as the benefit to the unemployed, could be increased by an extra allowance of £5.45 a week and, on reaching the final retirement age — 70 for a man and 65 for a woman — they may also receive an addition to their pension.

The very different philosophy underlying the treatment of the unemployed and the sick in the present British social security system emerges in many very different ways. Perhaps the best example is the very unequal treatment of earnings of the recipient and any adult dependant. You are allowed to work if you are ill but the work must either be under medical supervision as part of your treatment or 'work . . . which you have good cause for doing. Light work designed to keep your mind off your condition may be acceptable'. Earnings must ordinarily not exceed £15 a week, although this may be increased. This latter possibility could well be extended to the unemployed, particularly the long-term unemployed, to help maintain their self-respect and prevent physical deterioration with the aimless passing of time. But the unemployed are not allowed to earn any more than 75p per day *before* tax. Reasonable expenses may be deducted, but over 75p you lose your benefit for that day; and there are three other restrictions on this too. Earnings by an adult dependant are also treated differently. The wife of a man on invalidity pension, for example, will still receive the full increase as a dependant provided that she earns no more than £45 a week; above that the addition will be reduced gradually. In contrast, the wife of an unemployed man may only earn £12.75 a week before she loses the whole increase. In the extreme and probably unlikely case where both adults earn their maximum entitlement, a couple with two children may receive a mixture of earnings and benefit up to £114.60 while the worker is sick but only £52.10 while unemployed before benefit is affected.

There have been suggestions that the additional expenditure on the sick has led some social security offices to treat claims for invalidity benefit particularly toughly. One recent case is particularly disturbing, although I do not know how typical it is. In his late forties and married with four children, one disabled man had worked for over ten years for the local authority in the same job. After six months off work on sickness benefit, he was examined by an independent consultant who pronounced him fit 'for light work'. None of the departments in the local authority had a suitable job, and he was given notice. He was disallowed invalidity benefit and appealed. The welfare rights worker presented a supporting letter from the man's own doctor that said: 'I do not think any employer would employ him for nothing . . . in such a state of health'. One independent report requested by the tribunal from a consultant psychiatrist concluded that the man was 'only able to undertake work which does not involve any lifting, climbing, walking a great deal or use of speech and coming in contact with many people. In other words the job will almost have to be tailor-made for him. It is unlikely that there will be any material change in his condition in the foreseeable future'. At an appeal in mid-1980, after further Medical Officers' reports that the man was fit for work within much the same limits, the tribunal allowed the appeal adding that

> the question of whether he could do any remunerative work should be looked at realistically and the decision should take into account the difficulty of anyone so disabled as claimant being employed. He was found unfit to work for the council, a job he had had as a disabled man and he had been turned down by Remploy and Light Industries, both of whom employed disabled persons. In spite of the medical evidence the tribunal do not consider he is fit for any work.

During the period the man had been disallowed sickness benefit and required to register for work, he had not been able to obtain a doctor's certificate, while his claim for benefit was pending appeal. It took further correspondence and a request for another appeal before the due payment was made.

The differences between the benefits for invalids and unemployed and their implications have been spelt out at some length simply because the increasing multiplicity of benefits and their constant uprating, plus growing public discussion about high public expenditure on social security benefits, serve to disguise the very different provisions and opportunities available to different categories in our social security system. While sickness merits continuing support, we have decided as a society that people who are suffering prolonged unemployment no longer merit support because of their *unemployment.* They can only claim a state benefit because they are *poor* as well as unemployed, and so qualify for supplementary benefit. With increasing unemployment the failure of the insurance system has forced more and more people to do this. When the supplementary benefits scheme was introduced in 1966, one third of the men registered unemployed were supported by it, but at the last four annual counts the proportion has been one half or higher. Considerably more men and any dependants have been receiving help from 'the safety-net' of supplementary benefits than from the basic insurance scheme intended as the first line of defence against unemployment.

Supplementary benefit is paid on a very different basis to the insurance benefit. The allowances are made according to the 'need' of the unemployed person and any dependants after taking account of their 'resources'. How the 'need' is calculated and what counts as 'resources' are now laid down in the Social Security Act 1980 and its regulations. If the insurance benefit and any other income fall below the 'need' level, then both benefits may be received. There are no contribution conditions for supplementary benefit, but it may be reduced, limited in duration, refused or stopped even if the official criteria of need are met but certain other conditions are not (for a more detailed analysis of the operation of these controls, see M.J. Hill, 1980b; CPAG, 1981).

The 'scale rate' or current level of supplementary benefit

for a married couple where the normal wage-earner is out of work is £34.60; for a person living alone it is £21.30. Rent and rates are usually paid as well, or an allowance to owner-occupiers including rates and the interest, but *not* capital repayments on a mortgage. Flat-rate insurance benefit has never been set well above the basic supplementary benefit level, including rent, and so families tend to receive a higher income from supplementary benefit than from flat-rate insurance by itself, especially as children receive a higher amount on supplementary benefit according to their age. Others remain at much the same level and only a few actually receive less. Indeed, it is pointed out, many unemployed are quite unclear as to which benefit they are receiving.

The distinction between insurance benefit and supplementary benefit is regarded as insignificant by many, and there are rumours that the Rayner enquiry into benefits for the unemployed may effectively replace both schemes by a simpler means-tested scheme. However, the distinction between the two benefits is very important. For example, a married man is entitled to insurance benefit for himself, however great the earnings of his wife. In calculating their entitlement to supplementary benefit only £4 of her earnings, net of expenses, may be ignored. Given that unemployment amongst women has risen very much faster over the last decade and that many more are experiencing prolonged registered unemployment, it is all the more important that a woman cannot qualify for supplementary benefits when she is unemployed if her husband is in work. 'Equal treatment' introduced under new legislation enables a couple to choose which member should be regarded as the major wage-earner and so able to claim supplementary benefit. But since men's wages tend to be very much higher than women's, it is very unlikely that many wives will be able to draw supplementary benefit, although for the first year they may be entitled to insurance benefit if they have paid the full contributions. Finally, any capital or income received do not affect compensation through insurance benefit, except earnings or pay in lieu of notice. Very little income received is ignored or 'disregarded' in claims for supplementary benefit. In addition, a much lower cut-off point of £2,000 has now been imposed on the capital that claimants may hold. So anyone who put a redundancy payment – the compensation for a loss of a job earned over the years – of more than £2,000 into savings for their retirement or any other future need would not be eligible for any supplementary benefit.

The distinction between the two systems of benefit is bound to become even more marked with the implementation of the 1980 Social Security Act, the biggest revision in the system for over thirty years at least. This follows an intensive internal review of the workings of the system that offered a range of proposals for discussion. But the whole review exercise was quite simply nobbled at an early stage by the imposition of the requirement that the total changes proposed should be achieved at 'no cost'. The package that was eventually enacted by the new government was rushed into effect at the time of the benefit uprating in November 1980, and it is not yet clear how it is operating in practice. The Act itself was generally more negative and less directed to improving the living standards of claimants or simplifying the scheme for them (rather than for officials).

Despite the emphasis on a revised and more intelligible legal structure, which reduces the extent of discretion, there is still plenty of opportunity for discretion 'largely to give less rather than more' (*New Society,* 20 November 1980). For example, for some years single special payments have been made for items such as clothing and footwear, particularly for children. These have provided a small but important way of raising the standard of living of families on benefits that the government itself, as well as the Supplementary Benefits Commission, has declared are inadequate for families. Official as well as independent studies have documented the harsh poverty among families dependent upon supplementary benefit, but the new scheme seeks to restrict severely the allocation of these special grants, very largely on the grounds that previous distribution was both arbitrary and excessive. The new scheme was put into effect with such haste that staff generally only received a week's training for the quite major changes, and the regulations themselves were drafted at considerable speed. It is already becoming evident that the criteria for allocation of the special grants under the new system are

far from simple. Officers have, for example, to exercise their
own judgement or discretion as to whether the wearing out
of an item is due to normal wear and tear or some special
need. The Chief Benefit Officer's Notes of Guidance are said
to distinguish between the ordinary scuffing and wearing out
of children's shoes and clothing, which would have to be replaced from the weekly grant, and damage that could occur
if, for example, a child fell out of a tree. No doubt some of
the more scroungerphobic newspapers and MPs will be pro-
ducing stories of a new form of child-battering to obtain a
special grant!

One major and undeniable advance in the new scheme is
that the higher long-term benefit, which raises the weekly
benefit by 25 per cent, is now paid to all claimants under
retirement age after one rather than two years on benefit.
But there is still one exception: unemployed claimants continue not to be entitled to this higher rate. Despite all the
evidence that has been collected by and is available to the
government about the greater needs of the long-term unemployed and their higher risk of poverty, our social security
system continues to discriminate against them in two ways.
First, they are thrown off the insurance scheme after a year,
and then they are only accorded second-class status as long-
term recipients of supplementary benefit. Both Labour and
Conservative governments have refused to extend the higher
long-term benefit to the unemployed, even when the proposals had had the full support of the DHSS's own review
team and the Supplementary Benefits Commission. The extra
cost would be some £65 million a year, which is a very small
amount indeed set against the substantial amounts of tax for-
gone as a result of the growing number of fringe benefits and
company perks to those in generally better-paid jobs.

Help for the unemployed is hedged around with more constraints and limitations than for most claimants. The uneasy
mixture of support and control makes dealing with the variety
of complex problems that the unemployed bring a much
more awkward and burdensome chore for both staff and
claimant. As a result the unemployed take up much more
time and staff costs than the retired, who make up the majority
of social security customers. With the great increase in appli-

cants, the difficulties of applying a hurriedly worked out and
– as is becoming increasingly evident – complex scheme are
likely to lead to even shorter shrift or simple rule-of-thumb
handling of claimants. Although the staff unions have taken
an important initiative in calling attention to the deterioration
in service, encouraged partly by the threat of staff cuts and
certainly by the failure to increase numbers in relation to
demand, the old tradition among many staff of 'when in
doubt, pay nowt' may well gain strength again. The strain
under which officers have had to operate has already been
made clear in a confidential report leaked to *New Society*
(10 July 1980). The experience of a higher civil servant,
seconded for a few months to one local office, reveals very
disturbing evidence of how pressure and confusion can lead
to harsher treatment of those seen as less deserving, including
the unemployed.

Against the growing evidence of a system that deteriorates
as it attempts to offer a catch-all service when it was intended
to provide occasional help as a safety-net for the few who fell
through insurance systems, the present government's attempt
to crack down on scroungers by doubling the number of
Unemployment Review Officers is clearly very much more
worrying. Acting 'in the interests both of claimants and public
accountability' (SBC, 1979, p.50), UROs are expected to
keep all unemployed claimants 'under review', sending them
letters and interviewing them on their efforts to find work.
Although no doubt many can play a helpful role and provide
useful advice, the lack of jobs simply forces them to be 'cost
effective' by 'shuffling the pack', as many UROs themselves
describe their work. The confidential report revealed the
scope for 'frightening a claimant . . . UROs are out to secure
savings (again the ultimate measure of their success) and in
the absence of better facilities [or jobs], vague encouragement . . . and specific threats are all they have' (*New Society*,
10 July 1980).

Given the increasing unemployment with a sharp rise in
prolonged unemployment that will follow, it is all the more
depressing that 'those whose unemployment results from a
severely disadvantaged position in the labour market . . .
become the prime concern of the organisation which has taken

over the legacy of the Poor Law'. By contrast, the shorter term unemployed and those simply seeking to change jobs get 'the benefit of all the modern developments in methods of counselling, placing and training for employment' (M.J. Hill, 1974, p.14). These comments in 1974 must carry all the more weight since Mr Prentice as Minister for Social Security has placed so much emphasis on the role of the URO in checking fraud and saving tax payers' money.

In recent years the Supplementary Benefits Commission has made many efforts to draw government and public attention to the needs of the long-term unemployed and of those faced with the choice of inadequate benefits or low pay in often quite appalling jobs. Yet no research has been undertaken to establish what happens to those people who cease to claim benefit after receiving a letter from or being seen by the URO. We do not know whether they are able to find good and secure jobs or are forced into temporary, poor-paying and unpleasant ones only to return to the dole queue in a few months. It is believed that some may no longer be able to cope with the strain of unemployment and the fear of losing benefit, and end up in a mental hospital or perhaps prison — which of course is only transferring the public expenditure charge to another section of the accounts. But to fail to identify the social and human price of such 'cost-effective' measures, when long-term unemployment has been rising and benefits have been cut and restricted, must be seen as a particularly shameful mark on the record of the Supplementary Benefits Commission.

It is in this climate that one must examine any claims that a solution, at least in part, to the decline in employment opportunities can be found in the 'informal' or 'hidden' economy. However attractive and satisfying informal work within the community may be in combating the burden of 'enforced leisure', the development is 'very dangerous' to the unemployed (TUSIU, 1980, p.31). It will push them still further into the marginal world where they are forever under threat from 'authority'. The expansion of social security fraud inspectors will be legitimated. The attacks on the 'scroungers with two colour TVs' will be intensified. This is already beginning to be used to justify talk of further cuts in benefits:

the unemployed, it is said, need less public support because of their profitable activities in the irregular economy. The final result will actually be to push the unemployed into such work in order to survive, and prosecutions of their non-declaration of earnings will only justify a further crackdown. In fact we do not know the extent to which the unemployed are involved in this informal or black economy. The various aggregate statistics of this that are produced are very rough guesstimates, and we do not know what proportion of this undeclared income comes from those in work who are moon-lighting — for example, electricians or plumbers carrying out repairs in the evenings or at weekends — without declaring this on their tax returns. But it fits more easily with public attitudes towards the unemployed to hold this group more responsible for the loss of tax revenue that results.

One small study by David Binns of Middlesex Polytechnic on a Glasgow housing estate found very little evidence of any informal and undeclared earnings that exceeded the earn-ings allowed. 'The most exciting cases appeared to consist of a bit of electric meter tampering, with child minding and cleaning forming the mainstay of cash jobs on the side' (Aileen Ballantyne in *The Guardian,* 18 November, 1980). But the stories of major enterprises providing significant extra income continued to flourish on anecdotal evidence, giving additional support to those who argue that benefits are so generous that they reduce the incentive to find work.

The DHSS group reviewing the supplementary benefit system examined this issue and reported that 'the proportion of the unemployed who actually get more money in benefit than in work is very small' (quoted in SBC, 1980, p.39). They tended to be those only recently out of work receiving the maximum benefits including earnings-related supplement and probably a tax rebate as well 'when the disincentive effects seem small anyway; or men on supplementary benefit with low earnings potential and large families.' These are 'among the poorest on supplementary benefit and many of them are in poor health and have other personal problems.' (ibid.). These conclusions are supported by other research which confirms that these men do not set unrealistic wage levels in their search for work and shows the very limited number and quality of jobs available to those with few skills, especially in the areas of higher unemployment.

Obviously there are some people who are reluctant to find work, especially given the low pay and working conditions of many jobs available to them and there are others who fiddle their social security, just as there are people in jobs who do as little work as they possibly can or fiddle their income tax. There is no reason why the unemployed should be any different from the employed, but this is not to say that benefits are so generous that they discourage many from taking jobs (see Showler, 1980, pp.42–45). The real danger is that the beliefs in generous benefits and a growing army of scroungers will conceal the real effect of unemployment and poverty and prevent the rest of society from recognising the need to reduce unemployment and provide fairer compensation to its victims. Instead the victims become blamed for their continuing unemployment and the problem of unemployment is reduced in the view of many to a question of wilful idleness. The result is that there is more public support for doing something *to* the unemployed than *for* them.

CHAPTER 5

The Wider Impact

5.1 A JOBLESS SOCIETY

Attacks on the official figures of registered unemployment, with the charge that they seriously overstate the size of the problem, have tended to grow with high unemployment, especially while it is rising. Yet, ironically, this is the very time that unemployment is becoming more significant not only for a rapidly increasing number of people in the community, but also for society as a whole. In 1980 the combination of the swift rise in unemployment with predictions of further increases has meant that the official number out of work forms only a part of the total number whose lives are touched by the shadow of the recession.

A major failure in the current debate about high unemployment has been the inadequate attention given to this wider significance. There is a very powerful case that needs to be made much more explicitly and thoroughly against the acceptance of an economy operating with high unemployment. It is quite distinct from the economic costs of wasted labour and lost production, and encompasses far more than the hardship borne by those currently out of work, however severe and prolonged they are. Indeed this wider argument would retain considerable force and demand very much more attention than it has received even if the individual impact of unemployment were very much easier to bear than has been claimed in this book.

Full employment enables society to pursue many societal goals with much greater success than in a recession. At best, high unemployment slows down the progress towards these objectives; more commonly it may stop their achievement and even put them into reverse. It turns the publicly avowed pursuit of such objectives into a hypocrisy and a sham: it allows us to utter many worthy sentiments of concern but denies us the means of putting them into effect. What Murray Edelman (1964) has called 'the symbolic uses of politics' become an advanced art in many policy areas. We can continue to proclaim the goals and even pass legislation, but the effect will be minimal. Edelman's subsequent critique 'Words that Succeed and Policies that Fail' (1977) might have been designed for 'the workless state' that is replacing 'the welfare state'. We continue to give lip service to many objectives without fully acknowledging that they cannot effectively be pursued any longer with policies that were designed to work in an economy characterised by lasting low unemployment. There are very many ways in which the persistence of high unemployment devalues or debases the standard or quality of life in society in addition to increasing unemployment, and I can illustrate just a few of them here.

It is only when unemployment is treated as one aspect of problems in the world of work and in society as a whole that it becomes evident that many solutions to unemployment are hardly real answers at all. Early retirement or the extension of the school leaving age, for example, may reduce the official statistics of those out of work, but they do very little for those, young and old, who disappear from the unemployed count. The blinkered fixation on this single indicator of officially registered unemployed may lead many to claim a victory by the reduction of that visible and publicly debated measure. The problems of these groups are taken off the political agenda and so, to all intents and purposes, no longer exist.

Making The Best of a Bad Job

Higher unemployment not only affects the lives of those out of work and others kept out of the labour force, or hastened out of it. Many more who remain in work both are and feel much less secure and have to endure much greater uncertainty. Very many are suffering a cut in their earnings from the massive increase in short-time working and the unusually large reduction in overtime.

The fear of remaining unemployed or being laid off on the last-in—first-out basis from a new job reduces the mobility of workers when unemployment is high. Over the years, many larger firms and some small ones have moved towards internal promotion, taking recruits from outside the company at only certain positions on the occupational ladder. But for a very large proportion of the manual labour force the main way of getting a job that is more satisfying or rewarding is still to change employers. During periods of low unemployment most unemployment is brief and voluntary with workers moving up to these better jobs and so 'getting on'. With increasing unemployment, any move is much more risky because of the loss of security, and the cost in enduring deadening jobs or the frustration of ambitions becomes considerable. In North Tyneside during the increased unemployment of 1975 and 1976 1 in 3 men in work said that they had stayed in jobs to avoid the risk of unemployment by moving (North Tyneside CDP, 1978, pp.76 and 230).

This 'job stagnation' is only one way in which the workers' power is reduced during high unemployment. The chances of improving the quality or condition of a job are reduced and workers are liable to become trapped in less satisfying jobs. Ironically, therefore, unemployment helps to create a situation where cynical and dismissive stories about the unemployed are likely to flourish. Workers, frustrated and embittered by being forced to stay in their own unsatisfactory job, are all the more likely to believe stories of scroungers and fiddlers on the dole who escape from the tensions and pressures of employment that they find increasingly hard to bear.

Such disappointments and frustrations, sharpened by increasing deprivation, encourage scapegoating of outsiders and newcomers. 'Taking local jobs' has often been the charge directed at groups that are regarded as foreign to the local community. Tensions between Catholic and Protestant, black and white, become very much greater when jobs are scarce.

Workers who were prepared, if not happy, to see immigrant workers taking low-paid and unpleasant jobs when there was a labour shortage are much more likely to resent the British-born sons and daughters of these immigrants competing with their own children in a slack labour market. The National Front is encouraging these anxieties and fears, boasting of recruitment among school leavers. In the inner-city areas particularly hard hit by unemployment – and not only in London – they are claiming more and more successes with young unemployed who complain that 'the blacks' are the cause of unemployment. A recent issue of *Bulldog*, the paper of the Young National Front, was headlined 'We want jobs not more wogs'. This was the chant of their march through Nuneaton under the banner 'British jobs for British workers'. Earlier this year it carried a story on social security fraud headlined 'Black spongers' over another article headlined 'What about the White workers?' that reported that jobs and housing in different parts of London were being reserved for blacks. In August 1978 *Bulldog* reported that 'Britain's youth hate the multiracial society that the government is forcing them to live in!' 'They hate being forced to compete for jobs and houses with black foreigners. They HATE being treated as second class citizens in their own country!' (quoted a young recruit, 'I didn't think it was right that I couldn't get a job when there were blacks doing jobs I wanted to do. In Britain we should come first'). It is clear that this and other groups such as the more extreme British Movement are deliberately making use of increased unemployment to gain recruits among young labour force entrants, frustrated in their expectations of obtaining work.

This is not to say that problems such as racism are created simply by unemployment nor that full employment would lead to their disappearance. 'All these evils have their independent roots, but are inflated by unemployment and the fear of it' (Mason Gaffney, quoted in *Dissent*, 1976, p.137).

5.2   EQUAL OPPORTUNITY WITHOUT WORK?

One early victim of increased unemployment is liable to be the equal opportunity to gain work and to be treated equally in it. When demand for work far exceeds its supply, the weaker and less powerful members of society are the ones most likely to be excluded from the opportunity to work. We tend to talk of women and blacks, and in Northern Ireland of the Catholics, in the language of equal opportunity, but there are many others who are vulnerable and marginal. These include the young, the old, the disabled and handicapped, the immigrant and those leaving prison or mental hospital.

Equal opportunity in work is an aim that receives much verbal support. Indeed the near-unanimity of expressed support for some groups has itself often fostered the view that it is only a matter of time before the irrational prejudices of the bigoted minority give way and allow the objective to become an achievement. But a report to the Fair Employment Agency for Northern Ireland in September 1980 underlines the lessons of experience.

> Unless commitments to this goal from government, employers and the trade unions are followed by major positive actions, then equality of opportunity in employment will remain nothing more than a distant goal to which all can, when required, express sympathy. [Cormack *et al.*, 1980, p.64]

High unemployment lets governments, employers and others very much off the hook in bringing about the awkward changes that are necessary to eliminate discrimination and ensure equal opportunity. For one thing, the victims often help to reduce the visibility of the problem by making themselves scarce. Very many married women remain 'housewives' and stay among 'the silent reserve'; and many older workers accept the 'reality' and acquiesce in policies of early retirement or make no attempt to find the work they want after they pass the standard retirement age.

With fewer jobs available, gains by any one of the weaker groups are more likely to be achieved at the expense of others among those discriminated-against than by the exclusion of groups long established in the working population. Even within weaker groups, those already in work are better protected. Married women in their forties and fifties stay longer in the labour force, while unemployment increases among young women in their teens who lack both experience and qualifications.

The United States has had longer experience of attempting

to provide equal opportunity in employment and in protecting black or non-white groups from discrimination. In the 1960s there was substantial effort both through active manpower policies and through equal opportunity enactments to help black members of the labour force. Whether as a result of these measures, or of the stimulus to the economy provided by President Johnson's 1964 tax cut and the escalation of the war effort in Vietnam, the increase in employment helped to absorb many of the unemployed as well as the very large numbers coming into the labour force. Although gains fell short of what had been promised, let alone demanded, there were benefits to the black community, and these would probably have increased as unemployment was brought down further. But in the 1970s the United States suffered its worst unemployment since the 1930s, as we did in Britain, with dramatic increases to a rate of 8.5 per cent out of work in mid-1975. 'The gainers in the tight labor markets became the losers in the recession' (Levitan and Taggart, 1976). Lacking seniority and more concentrated in the less secure jobs, black workers were very vulnerable to losing their job. In six years the gap between white and black unemployment rose from 3 per cent to 6 per cent. White workers were also hard hit by the rapid deterioration in the labour market, and this had a second and very common effect. Rising unemployment erodes both the government's commitment to, and the wider public's support for, measures to take positive action in favour of less powerful groups.

Increased unemployment therefore brings a double blow to these groups. Not only does their insecure position in work leave them vulnerable when pay-offs occur and recruitment is cut back. There is also a weakening in general public sympathy to encourage a fairer deal for groups that are disadvantaged because they are regarded as less attractive for one reason or another by employers, trade unions and others who already have some power in the labour market. Those workers with long-established positions in the labour market naturally protest as their own jobs disappear, and their claims are vigorously put by the trade unions. It is not unusual to hear the seriousness of increased unemployment underlined by remarks such as 'it's not just the older worker/the unskilled/

the young out of work now' – and, in the United States, 'not just the blacks' or any other group with a tenuous hold at the bottom of the occupational hierarchy.

The importance of a tight labour market is vital in encouraging employers to take a more favourable view of those now regarded as more marginal members of the labour force. In the mid-1960s I visited eight countries in North America and Western Europe to collect evidence on the extent and problems of long-term unemployment and programmes being used to help. At that time, Sweden and particularly West Germany were suffering from severe labour shortages and they had absorbed many groups into their labour force that other countries were trying to take off their unemployment statistics and exclude from the labour force. In Germany in particular, considerable effort was being put into bringing the disabled into employment, whilst some other countries with particularly high unemployment had not even collected statistics on the proportion of these unemployed or on the employed who suffered from any disability. As I wrote at the time, 'Germany and the Scandinavian countries have pushed back the frontiers of unemployability over the last few years under the pressure of the scarcity of labour' (1968, p.36).

In Britain the employment services for the disabled have always held a very precarious position and in recent years their future has become increasingly uncertain. A quota system was introduced during the last war which requires employers to employ those on the official disabled persons' register. Any employer falling below the quota, which was fixed at 3% in 1946, is not supposed to hire a non-disabled worker without a permit from the employment service. The Disablement Resettlement Officers in job centres are expected to encourage employers to maintain their quota as well as give advice and guidance to both registered and non-registered disabled. The scheme was introduced at a time when labour was scarce and so the contribution of the disabled valued. The DROs have been encouraged to see their role in an educational light rather than in any policing way. In consequence there has been very great reluctance even to cajole or chivvy employers into meeting the quota, and permits appear to have been issued en masse. Large companies with multiple branches throughout the country need only obtain a block permit at their head office to enable them to escape the requirements of the quota throughout the whole of Britain, whatever the state of the local labour market.

This is a particularly good example of a programme to help to promote equal opportunities in the labour force whose philosophy was developed under the pressure of labour short-ages. The proportion of firms meeting the quota has dropped from two-thirds in the high employment years to one-third today. At present the only response of the government is to cut back even further on the service and maybe dismantle it altogether. Central government departments are not legally bound by the scheme although it is always said that they have accepted it — and certainly the Civil Service provides more opportunity than many manufacturing industries for the recruitment of disabled people. Yet only two government departments met the quota in June 1978. There is little official attempt to deny that many employers must have evaded the requirements of the quota without permits, but the number of prosecutions since the war has yet to reach double figures. Meanwhile the disabled remain particularly vulnerable to unemployment with rates amongst the regis-tered disabled twice the general average even during high unemployment. They are still more likely to be concentrated amongst the long-term unemployed, and so particularly exposed to the poverty that prolonged unemployment on low income brings.

After a review of the available evidence the Disability Alliance and Low Pay Unit concluded in 1979 that 'the spear-head of the government's policy on disabled employment has rusted through lack of use' (Jordan, 1979, pp.28–31). Not surprisingly, many more disabled have refused to go on the Disabled Persons' Register because they are convinced — often with good cause — that employers under no compulsion to take disabled prefer to recruit able-bodied workers when they have a choice of applicants. But many of these cannot conceal their disabilities, which are often combined with poor health, and they too are liable to higher and prolonged unem-ployment. The main groups of people who suffer through the unwillingness or inability of government to promote more equal protection and opportunity for the disabled are likely to be the less skilled and older workers with declining health in areas of particularly high unemployment. But, as the job market deteriorates, more and more people with some disability will find it harder to obtain work.

5.3 THE MEANING OF FULL EMPLOYMENT

The deepening gloom of the present economic crisis is encouraging far more exhortations that 'we must learn to live with unemployment'. With the anticipated or feared job destruction by micro-chips fast approaching us, the frequency of these strictures is probably even greater than it has been in other periods of rising unemployment. The combination of accelerating technological change and rising unemployment encourages such teaching, as the pre-automation scare of the early 1960s in the United States showed well. A central part of this catechism is, as I argued in the Introduction, that the days of full employment are over.

But have we ever had full employment? Outside wartime, certainly, I believe this widespread assumption is highly debatable. Full employment is not achieved just because the number of jobs available approximates to the number of unemployed. It is vital for future planning and discussions of policy to understand the inadequacies of this definition, however sophisticated and subtle the devices used to measure the numbers of jobs and people really available. Our failure to recognise this is but one more example of the way in which the study of policy in the world of work has fallen well behind that in other areas. The days are now past when civil servants would allow or even encourage enthusiastic Ministers of Housing to declare the end of homelessness or housing problems because the number of properties vacant exceeded the number of people needing a new home. But still the closeness between the lines indicating unemployed and vacancies on the monthly Department of Employment graphs continues to mesmerise discussion of the problem of unemployment. We all fall into this trap at one time or another because of the recurring need for simple clear indicators of the scale of a problem. The narrowing of the gap between the two lines is to be welcomed, but it does not mean that the problem has been solved. We do not know, without more information than the number of jobs and unemployed, whether the available workers have the right skills and relevant experience, and whether they live in the appropriate area for the jobs available; nor do we know whether the jobs have an adequate wage, offer decent working conditions and so on.

A fuller or social definition of full employment never seems to have been spelt out. That provided by William Beveridge in 1944 in his vigorous alternative report to the government White Paper on Employment Policy offers a valuable basis for discussion. After emphasising that full employment does not mean no unemployment at all, Beveridge argues that

> [full employment] means having always more vacant jobs than unemployed men, not slightly fewer jobs. It means the jobs are at fair wages, of such a kind, and so located that the unemployed men can reasonably be expected to take them; it means, by consequence, that the normal lag between losing one job and finding another will be very short. [1944, p.18]

'Jobs, rather than men, should wait' is Beveridge's most succinct summary, but his fuller explanation deserves quoting because I have been able to find very little discussion of the arguments for full employment in the British literature. Meanwhile the demand for full employment seems to have become ossified as some outdated catch-phrase of the post-war welfare state. It is easily dismissed as part of the rhetoric of opposition that trips much more lightly off the tongues of Labour Party leaders out of office. The *Daily Telegraph*'s caustic 'a ritual debate on unemployment' was applied to the House of Commons in the wicked days when unemployment climbed to 1 million under the Tories in the early 1970s. But it fits much of the fulminations of opposition MPs during recent debates just as well.

For Beveridge, the decisive argument for his definition of full employment was that

> difficulty in selling labour has consequences of a different order of harmfulness from those associated with difficulty in buying labour. A person who has difficulty in buying the labour he wants suffers

inconvenience or reduction in profits. A person who cannot sell his labour is in effect told that he is of no use. The first difficulty causes annoyance or loss; the other is a personal catastrophe. [Beveridge, 1944, p.19]

The underlying philosophy behind his definition is that for people 'to have value and a sense of value there must always be useful things waiting to be done, with money to pay for doing them'. Despite his traditional and conservative style, he is clearly under no illusion about what he sees as full employment and its significance for both the unemployed and the whole of society.

The labour market in the past has invariably, or all but invariably, been a buyer's market rather than a seller's market, with more unemployed men — generally many more unemployed men — than unfilled jobs. To reverse this and make the labour market always a seller's rather than a buyer's market, to remove not only unemployment but the fear of unemployment, would affect the work of many existing institutions. It would change and is meant to change fundamentally the conditions of living and working in Britain, to make Britain again a land of opportunity for all. [Beveridge, 1944, p.21]

Crucial emphasis is placed on the change from a buyer's market to a seller's market. This distinction is one of principle and entails a very different view of society and the purpose of life within it from those who argue that 'a short sharp dose of unemployment will bring us all to heel', as David Steel charges the present government (Liberal Party press release, 14 October 1980).

In many respects the definition that Beveridge offered is similar to the view of full employment that successive Swedish governments have sought to put into practice. It places particular emphasis on economic security, which goes much further than any concern with the overall level of unemployment. It is a social as well as an economic policy goal. Since the war, Sweden has certainly done much more than any other market economy to put into effect its claim that

full employment is the pillar of Swedish social policy . . . it starts as a concept of work, not as the sociologists of the fifties saw it, as a

necessary evil from which to escape to leisure time where the important things in life took place, but as a part of being human. If you
are unemployed or if your work is grim or terrible or hazardous that
will colour the rest of your existence. We see unemployment not
only as a gross economic waste, but as an individual human tragedy
because it deprives one of a meaningful social role. [Olaf Palme,
1977, quoted in Levison, 1980, p.144]

The meaning given to full employment by Beveridge and
Palme could be much more easily described as a worker's
definition rather than an employer's. As Michal Kalecki
declared in a lecture given in spring 1942, 'a first class political
issue is at stake here' (1943, p.324). Such differences, however, do not seem to have been given much explicit discussion
in Britain since the war. In the mid-1940s there would seem
to have been some national consensus behind such views,
even if one discounts the rosy, if not faintly pink, glow of
solidarity that many recollections and memoirs depict. But,
tragically, the low rate of unemployment that prevailed
throughout most of the next two decades made the discussion,
elaboration and improvement of ideas such as Beveridge ex-
pounded appear unnecessary. There were strong critics of his
position at the time, but the fairly muted debate quickly
slipped into discussion about what was the appropriate 'full
employment' level (Deacon, 1980b). The argument about the
level took more account of Beveridge's tentative suggestion
of 3 per cent and did not include any attempt to work out
whether his more extended definition could actually be given
any statistical form with the fairly crude tools used at that
time. The debate about full employment lapsed into a narrow
technical issue joined by relatively few economists and even
fewer others.

Meanwhile, the rest of the nation complacently assumed
the achievement of full employment and so the accomplish-
ment of one of the basic preconditions of what has come to
be called 'the welfare state', encouraged by increasing anxiety
over the shortage of labour. In January 1947 *The Times*
called for the 'selective immigration' of some half a million
foreign workers. In 1934 the economist Lionel Robbins had
argued that

an even sharper 'purge' would have been preferable to the 'lingering disease' brought about by governments introducing tariffs and relief measures, thereby preventing natural competitive forces from shaking out 'bad business' and setting the stage once more for business recovery. [Quoted in Showler, 1980, p.33]

By January 1947 Robbins was arguing that Britain needed to recruit some 100,000 foreigners into the pits if we were not 'to lapse into a position of impotence and economic chaos'. By the autumn there was even more urgent talk of an acute labour shortage and Clement Attlee pledged the government in the Commons to make an all-out attack on 'spivs and drones'. According to the *Daily Mail,* Scotland Yard would be used 'to help to round up the work-dodgers' and the drive would bring in at least 1½ million workers. The spivs were the 'wide-boys' epitomised by Arthur English, and the drones were 'either the "born tireds" or "the Duke's daughter" who is alleged to ride to hounds every day and dance throughout every night'. The Minister of Labour compared the two groups to eels and butterflies: 'Eels are slippery, and butterflies are hard to catch and not much use when you have caught them.' The extent of the concern is perhaps brought out most vividly by the official records, which reveal that in September the Labour Cabinet discussed banning the football pools to allow the redeployment of the women who processed the coupons into the chronically labour-starved textile industry (material used in this paragraph is drawn heavily from Deacon, 1980a,b and Showler, 1980).

In the early 1950s National Insurance and retirement were also a matter for concern but then attempts were being made to devise schemes to persuade workers to *defer* retirement as long as possible. Only seventeen years ago the National Economic Development Council drew attention to the importance of the considerable labour reserves in probably its best-known report, *Conditions Favourable to Faster Growth*: 'To draw these reserves into employment would make a substantial contribution to national employment and national growth' (1963, p.15). The swift change to anxiety over labour shortages with the apparent achievement of full employment with relatively little effort had the effect of convincing people that the economy had been mastered. There was no need therefore to examine the workings of the labour market in any detail or even to analyse how the new systems of benefits were operating. At the same time the importance of low unemployment to the development of social policy seemed to be so taken for granted that it became neglected. The world of work became isolated from the growth of 'the welfare state' services, and the need to examine the quality of work — its reward and satisfactions, the opportunities to make a career — was overlooked while standards for housing, education and health were being formulated.

CHAPTER 6

The Micro-Chip and the Economy

6.1 THE MICRO-ELECTRONIC REVOLUTION

For many people the whole purpose of this book, which is to restate the value of enabling all to contribute to the work of society, will seem grotesquely irrelevant as we enter the age of a technological revolution that they expect to transform virtually every aspect of our society. Instead, they are arguing, we need to be 'thinking the unthinkable' rather than dismissing 'the idea of a society where life without work is itself the norm' (Large, 1980).

There can be no doubt that the impact of micro-electronics may be profound, going well beyond limited occupational and industrial changes. Forester (1978) argues that the invention of the chip represents 'a quantum leap in technology far more important than the clumsy great computers of the 1950s'. He quotes one American authority:

> a good micro-computer of today, costing perhaps £150, has more computing capacity than the world's first large electronic computer. It is twenty times faster, has a larger memory, is thousands of times more reliable, consumes the power of a light bulb rather than that of a locomotive, occupies one-thirty-thousandth of volume and costs one-tenthousandth as much. It is available by mail order or can be bought across the counter.

The cost of the new technology has been falling at a dramatic rate, at the same time as micro-chips have been improved and so become more productive. 'The use of chips makes possible massive savings in energy consumption, maintenance, testing, floor space and back-up facilities' (Forester, 1978).

It is hardly surprising, therefore, that its advent is described dramatically — for example, an 'information revolution' or a 'tidal wave of electronics'. Its effect on employment is described in equally vivid terms and in West Germany the microprocessor has been called 'the job killer'. Forester describes the official French government Nora report as showing 'how the micro-processor will *wreak havoc* on the existing industrial structures, by *attacking* jobs in the existing information sectors like banking and (thanks to the industrial robot) by *destroying* jobs in manufacturing too' (my emphasis).

Many other responses, by contrast, appear not cool or dispassionate but more akin to trying to put out a nuclear holocaust with a damp fire-blanket. Some counter-critics scarcely manage to conceal their yawns as they report that we have heard it all before. And in many ways we have. For years, science fiction has both fed on and nourished the idea of a society where work will no longer be necessary or where some form of robot or automated and programmed product has enslaved us all. The very vividness of fantasies may help to weaken or distract us from facing up to possible realities. But there is also the vulnerability of prediction: those who over-reacted last time may be all the more inclined to take a too conservative view this time.

In the late 1950s and early 1960s Britain never really experienced the ferocity of many of the American predictions about the impact of the computer. The imminence of the 'cybernetic revolution' in the early 1960s amid rising unemployment and much increased general concern about the efficiency of America's economy led many distinguished writers and social scientists into apocalyptic visions of a new automated and workless society in well-publicised paperbacks. It is open to debate how much this was the result of the escalation of the war in Vietnam or just of greater investment in high technology defence, how much it was the result of President Johnson's 1964 tax cut or of changes in the international economy, but, by the time much of their writing reached the bookstalls, the American economy had begun to absorb labour so fast that many of the authors would probably have preferred to see their efforts remaindered in the science fiction section for better chance of a sale.

The mistaken predictions by no means go one way only. In 1886 the United States Commissioner of Labour stated in his First Annual Report that 'the era of rapid industrial advance had ended for the civilised world . . . Some new processes of manufacture could be expected, he said, and these would act as an ameliorating influence, but the main task remaining was that of consolidating and utilising the great technical discoveries of the 19th century!' (quoted by Seymour Wolfbein in OECD, 1965).

The agony of the uncertainty is made all the greater by the fact that the electronic revolution offers not only great potential for the disturbance of society but also promises great opportunities. The causes, or excuses, that lead to the exclusion of many older or less physically able people from participating more actively in society and from contributing to it might well be removed by the new technological changes. Many of the most boring and physically demanding and dangerous jobs could be carried out by industrial robots. The size of the new product and its limited demand for energy could enable much greater mobility of work. The first Industrial Revolution tied the development of manufacturing physically close to sources of energy, power and materials. It also encouraged the creation of vast workforce units. The light micro-chip frees people to work in their own homes or as they move around, and enables them to be very much more productive. The sheeplike processions of the daily rush hour and the concentration of workers in dirty and deafening factories could be abolished. Quick and easy access to information with micro-computer terminals in the home, coupled with the development of the word-processor, may help to abolish much deadening routine non-manual work to which very many women are now subject in the male-dominated world of the office.

Tom Stonier (1979) suggests that 'it is highly probable that by early in the next century it will require no more than 10% of the labour force to provide us with all material needs, that is, all the food we eat, all the clothes we wear, all the textiles, appliances etc.' Benefiting from the enormous advances in information technology, we shall be able to move to the 'new productive systems, which require greater mental and less manual effort'. There will be more opportunity for creativity and innovation in our work. Greater importance will be given to the exchange of services between individuals and within a community. Freed from the office or factory, we shall no longer have to break the day up into long exhausting hours of labour followed by others in which we have little energy for our leisure or are forced into the unwaged labour of housework in the home. In this optimistic view, work can become a better integrated part of our lives, providing greater intrinsic satisfaction and reward and not just the means to survive or entertain ourselves outside working hours.

But long before we drift into dreams or nightmares about these sharply contrasting futures, we ought to consider some very awkward questions about the extent of change that is likely and the speed with which it may occur. Technological change has been a common and important part of life in an industrial society like ours for at least the last two centuries. There is also, as William Beveridge pointed out in 1909, 'a very common criticism of the existing industrial order' that 'places the root cause of unemployment in the supersession of men by machines' (1909, p.8). Such a bogey-man is all the more convenient to governments and the established powers within society when others are suffering increased unemployment and there is generally rising dissatisfaction with the management of the economy. In the United States, the Report of the National Commission on Technology, Automation and Economic Progress commented dryly after unemployment had fallen, 'the high unemployment that led to the formation of this Commission [in August 1964] was the consequence of passive public policy, not the inevitable consequence of the pace of technological change' (1966, p.15). There are clearly parallels with the present day in Britain, although some of us would hardly describe the permissive non-interventionism that allows unemployment to rise as a 'passive' policy. Indeed, the obvious inactivity of the Conservative government may help to account for an apparent reduction in panic over the advent of the micro-chip. It certainly seems to be recognised that technological change does not provide any explanation or excuse for current levels of unemployment.

Among those who have carried out a more detailed study of its likely impact, neither the MSC nor the Manpower Research Group of the University of Warwick anticipates any major impact until the second half of this decade. In its 1980 *Manpower Review*, the MSC adds 'even in the longer term we have not seen the micro-processor as transforming the demand for labour but as only one factor in the uncertain environment' (1980, p.24). In defending what they describe as a 'moderate' view — or ostrich-like as many others would see it — they admit that

the technical possibility obviously exists . . . but what is technically possible is not bound to happen — or at least is unlikely to happen in the short time scale that is often hypothesised. It takes time for innovations to be introduced and to spread throughout industry. [p.24]

They place much weight on the argument that previous advances in technology have generally resulted in an increasing demand for labour, although of course there may well be a marked shift in the type of labour that is demanded. With the advent of the computer, for example, there was a dramatic change in the type of jobs demanded in banking, commerce and many office industries. One major effect was to encourage the development of a dual labour market within many firms. There was a great growth in many very routine non-manual jobs, which were carried out, often on a part-time basis, by the married women who were entering the labour force in increasing numbers. Meanwhile the more technical and highly skilled or managerial jobs with better pay and career prospects remained with men.

This time it appears that it may well be many of the new clerical jobs that were created in the first computer revolution that will disappear with the dramatic changes in the information industry. While some studies have been predicting a rise in female employment of 1 million over this decade with little more than 100,000 extra jobs for men, many more analysts are emphasising that it is the 'heartland' of women's employment that is most threatened by technological advances through word-processors and other units in the office. At the same time, industrial robots and other forms of automatic assembly will remove many of the lower-paid manufacturing jobs where female manual workers tend to be concentrated.

The success of other countries in already coping with the initial impact is both encouraging and worrying. On the one hand it provides some hard evidence of the actual way in which the advent of micro-electronics is affecting employment and society as a whole. 'Japan might be regarded as five years ahead of Britain in the exploitation of the silicon chip and has a negligible unemployment problem' (MSC, 1980, p.24). In the United States, which has also moved much further and faster into using the new technology, 'employment rose by some 10 million in the two years after 1975' (CSE–LWG, 1980, p.55). These and other illustrations encourage the view that 'the argument for imminent, prolonged and large scale employment loss thus runs against historical experience, economic theory and the current experience of more technologically advanced economies abroad' (MSC, 1980, p.24). But for many people this evidence is itself worrying. The great danger stressed, for example, by the TUC is that we may fail to invest adequately and speedily enough in new developments so that other countries reap the benefits of the new technology. In consequence we will lose far more jobs because British productivity will not rise sufficiently and we will be even less able to compete in international markets. If, however, we can improve our productivity, then the increased demand that this may stimulate could help to absorb jobs lost by the introduction of the new technology.

> Even on the most pessimistic assumptions . . . it is estimated that new technology will displace some 4 million jobs over the next fifteen years. This figure is equivalent to a rise in productivity of 1% a year, which can be compared with an average rise in productivity of 2% over the last twenty years. [CSE–LWG, 1980, p.55]

The force of this evidence is to shift the argument away from the technological determinism underlying many of the predictions of greatest gloom. Instead we need to look much more closely at the political and industrial issues. How willing are employers and employees to make use of the new technology and how quickly can they do it? The Equal Opportunities Commission's study of office automation found many women were attracted by the possibility of using word-processors to ease much of the repetitive drudgery of typing and to enable them to switch to part-time work or more flexible working hours. It was their employers who were more reluctant to undertake the major reorganisation of the office that this would require (Large, 1980). Equally, however, in what ways will workers and their trade unions react to demands to adapt or discard long-established working practices and patterns of working relationships? There is often a tendency to make adaptations in order to secure the jobs of those currently employed rather than to accept wholesale changes.

It becomes evident that the major changes that technological innovations may require to enable them to be used most effectively — improving both the quality and the productivity of the job — could be delayed while government, employers and workers argue over who bears the burden. Any change of this scale is 'a field for struggle'. Under the pressure of already rising unemployment, workers may be expected to take particularly defensive positions towards many persuasive attempts at change.

The outlook is most bleak where technological advance and some form of the current non-interventionist government policies are maintained together. In a society 'chipped' and 'monetarised' beyond recognition, unemployment would be likely to soar well beyond the 5 million forecast in *The Collapse of Work* (Jenkins and Sherman, 1979). This prospect makes it all the more urgent that measures be taken to tackle the rising problem of unemployment and the persisting issue of the distribution of the available work in society before the full impact of the micro-electronic revolution is upon us. If we do not act, we may continue our current decline until, unprepared and uncompetitive, de-industrialisation and de-skilling hit the British labour force as North Sea oil runs out.

6.2   UNEMPLOYMENT AND THE ECONOMY

While the micro-chip poses both a challenge and a threat for the future, the underlying causes of our present high levels of unemployment have to be sought elsewhere. What has struck this non-economist trying to pick his way through the battle-lines of the various established positions is how much easier it is to attack others' explanations and reject their proposals than it is to make a detailed case for one's own alternatives. Most analysts are much more at ease in putting the blame on others' past policies than in clearly identifying the long-term underlying causes of our present economic decline and distinguishing them from the more immediate developments and policies that have precipitated the current acute crisis. Finally, many analysts distinguish the general problems of the economy from the issue of unemployment and show little interest in, or expectation of, reducing the numbers out of work very much. There is very little discussion of specific help for those who will remain out of work and no significant discussion at all about achieving a more equal distribution of unemployment if that is the price 'we' have to pay.

Many of the possible long-term causes can be studied much more easily in a comparative context, although this has been little attempted. Detailed analysis across nine industrial countries shows wide differences in the impact of general world recession and in particular of the sharp increase in oil prices. A comparative examination also helps to remove some of the stock explanations for the higher unemployment in Britain. Many countries have had much faster increases in teenagers and married women entering the labour force, as well as slower rates of growth in productivity, without as high an increase in unemployment since 1960. Between 1960 and 1978 the United Kingdom had one of the lowest growth rates in civilian employment – and by 1990 it will have dropped even further behind (Sorrentino, 1980). Only low growth in the gross domestic product appears to have distinguished us from many other industrial countries (see also Dean, 1979).

This does not, however, prevent a combination of these different factors from creating particular problems in Britain, and there is a tendency for many people to put the blame on the high employment years of the early 'welfare state'. There are frequent references to some

> English disease . . . a national malaise, a form of political sclerosis brought on by the exertions of war and the compulsive search for comfort and security that followed it . . . we are taxed to death and molly-coddled into the grave . . . [Mackenzie, 1958, p.15]

Clearly the molly-coddling and penal taxation are seen as part of a massive state intervention during the twenty years after the war before we began to reap the harvest of increasing unemployment in the mid-1960s. Somehow or other, all the problems seen to derive from that period become related, and a significant part of the blame is attributed to the interfering, hyperactive state of the Butskellite or paternalistic Macmillan model. The slow increases in productivity and adaptability to technological change, limited labour mobility and more restrictive practices, growing trade union power — at least on the shop floor — and tougher collective bargaining believed to create an inflationary wage-spiral are presented as the results of *failing* to allow the market to operate. Even the seeds of 'crowding out' (where, despite all the evidence, growth in the public sector, especially the social services, is alleged to deprive private manufacturing industry of the labour needed to develop) are found in this period. And these are just some of the factors that are believed to make present policies of tight monetary control and public expenditure cuts essential for our economic recovery.

One of the most curious facts of the low unemployment years of the 1950s and early 1960s is that, beyond some efforts to affect aggregate demand at a national level, there was very little in the way of interventionist policies at all. It is very much easier to mount an argument that the mis-match of labour that began to occur was due to successive governments assuming that full employment had been achieved, very largely at their own doing. They believed that this constituted a sufficient economic and industrial policy to enable the many necessary changes to be made. During this period, active intervention in the labour market virtually ceased.

There was, for example, very little attempt, if any, to tackle the problems of the widening regional imbalance of supply and demand. The forms of demand management attempted nationally helped to reduce unemployment faster in regions of labour shortage than in the more remote regions with higher unemployment. Industrial training was very largely left to companies, with the result that we failed to develop the capability to make full use of technological changes in the early 1960s, let alone today, and particularly overlooked the need for training at higher technical and managerial levels, which was developing in many other European countries. Then, as later, little effort was made to counter or moderate the increasing power of the growing number of multinational companies, which are now said to exercise a particularly dominant influence on the British economy.

As many observers have pointed out, the major distinction in public policy between Britain and other European countries in the post-war period was the failure to encourage long-term investment in industry. The Bank of England was nationalised in 1946 but, as *Business Week* (14 March 1977) pointed out, 'it received a mandate to supervise the financial community within the City without interference from Whitehall'. As a result there was no long-term shift in the investment policies of the City, which 'had traditionally served as the centre of the British Empire and of international financial transactions rather than as the co-ordinator of domestic economic growth' (Levison, 1980, p.122). Even with the more active but short-lived attempts of the Labour government's Department of Economic Affairs, active policies to encourage investment and to gain the support of the trade unions and employers in promoting the necessary industrial changes remained extremely limited throughout the 1960s. The Conservative government of the early 1970s attempted to dragoon the trade unions into industrial cooperation by 'launching the most aggressive attack on Trade Unions ever attempted in any post-war period' while the parliament in 'free market' Germany was preparing legislation to give the trade unions more co-determination with management in the major industries. In his analysis of post-war policies to maintain employment, Andrew Levison emphasises how not only

Sweden, but Germany and France, had governments that took a more active role in the economy while Britain, despite its 'welfare state' rhetoric, largely confined itself to 'conventional physical and monetary actions and under the Tories direct government commitment to the ideal of laissez faire' (Levison, 1980, p.129 and Ch. 4 generally).

In the more acute and immediate crisis of today there appears to be increasing agreement that Conservative monetarism has failed to meet its own objectives of controlling the money supply and cutting the public sector borrowing requirement, despite massive cuts in the social services. At the same time the government has allowed, if not forced, unemployment to rise at a dramatic rate so that even former supporters of its policies among industrialists speak of the 'erosion of our industrial base'. This will make it very much more difficult for us to take advantage of any easing of the world recession. At the same time of course, as this book has argued, there has been a massive cost borne by society and in particular by the unemployed. Only part of the economic cost to those out of work is compensated by transfer payments, but these appear in the total of public expenditure making it even more difficult for the Conservatives to restrict its growth. Despite the 5 per cent cut in benefits in November 1980, the phasing-out of the earnings-related supplement by 1982 and the savings expected under the new Social Security Act, clearly some of the concern about this public cost fuels further resentment and helps to preserve the stigma of the unemployed.

There can be little doubt that unemployment would have risen under the policies of the previous Labour government, which also gave priority to tackling inflation at the expense of the unemployed. We do not know how they would have coped with the panicky doubling of oil prices with the Iranian Revolution in 1979, even when oil was not in short supply. The effect was to deepen the recession all the more for Britain because of the 'oil-dictated strength of sterling' and its effect on exports (*Guardian,* 9 December, 1980). But the Conservative removal of exchange controls in 1979 and maintenance of high interest rates are both creating difficulties. Given recent figures, which show that nearly £1 billion of capital was sent abroad in the third quarter of 1980 – more than double previous quarters — it would appear that the City is still failing to direct any long-term investment to help the adaptation and modernisation of British industry. Meanwhile, the high interest rates are forcing many companies to increase their borrowing even at current rates. These have pushed up the value of sterling in relation to other currencies and attracted considerable foreign speculative funds. Seeking short-term gains rather than long-term returns from industrial investment, they too have increased the money supply within Britain. At the same time the higher interest rates make efforts to increase or even maintain exports very much more difficult as we become less competitive in international markets.

The axing of government support for industrial training boards and the lack of sustained and consistent industrial and regional polices are further evidence of its anti-interventionist position. 'Jobs will create themselves if we allow them to', Sir Keith Joseph said on television in October 1980. Meanwhile, 'non-interventionism' increasingly appears as a positive measure against the unions and a barely disguised form of incomes policy, now supported by the 6 per cent control on labour costs in local government. 'No man is an island. Your pay increase might be someone else's job', Mrs Thatcher told the full General Council of the TUC in her first meeting with them after eighteen months as Prime Minister. The Chancellor of the Exchequer hammered home the same message during the 1980 Conservative Party Conference when he argued that management should realise that a 4 per cent cut in their wages bill would bring in five times more than a 4 per cent cut in interest rates.

The reduction, if not destruction, of trade-union and worker powers to resist is, of course, welcomed by those who see them as largely or primarily responsible for our present economic troubles. By inflated wage demands, it is argued, they are pricing themselves out of jobs as well as pushing up inflation for the whole of society. One long-term critic, if not opponent, of the trade unions marching us all down the *Road to Serfdom* is Friedrich Hayek. Seen by many as an architect of monetarism, he has recently returned to his attack on the unions in a pamphlet for the Institute of Economic

Affairs. Many of the 'legalised powers of the unions . . . are the prime source of unemployment. They are the main reason for the decline of the British economy in general' (quoted in *Daily Mail,* 1 December 1980). But the increasing rise in the exchange rate would seem to have contributed much more to the loss of competitiveness for British exports than any increase in wages. The evidence that wage-push inflation is largely the cause of our present economic problems is very doubtful (Showler, 1980, pp.37—42 and 54—8). The gains from depressing wage demands by a massive increase in unemployment are not at all evident and may in the long run make employer—employee relations far worse, embittering collective bargaining and alienating the unions.

The problem facing those who would advocate some Alternative Economic Strategy is that any expansion might well lead to an increase in imports, because British industry has been traditionally slow to respond to any stimulus. In addition, it has been all the more severely affected by the current recession. Import controls have long been proposed by such groups as the Cambridge Economic Policy Group but evoke a very negative reaction from others. Yet many different quotas already exist on nearly all textile imports and there are various informal agreements such as the one with Japan on car imports. Given the particular need to provide industry with time to recover from the recession (made worse by the impact of monetarism with high interest and exchange rates), some form of controlled growth or stabilisation of imports generally would seem to be needed.

Arguments rage equally, if not more, ferociously over the merits of income policies and how they might be operated. The concern of this book is with the containment and then sustained reduction of unemployment. This cannot, it appears even more evidently today, be achieved by non-interventionist policies. The role of economic and social planning seems all the more crucial if the move to much lower levels of unemployment is to be carried out in such a way that the very unequal distribution of unemployment is to be reduced and that those who bear the cost are more justly compensated. It does not seem possible that these changes can be brought about without some form of intervention in the distribution of income and wealth. The problem is to develop and gain acceptance for the policies that would be necessary.

The purpose of this book is not to provide detailed economic policy proposals, which I am not qualified to do, but to spell out both the significance of unemployment and the argument for fighting it with greater determination. An important part of that argument is the massive economic and social cost to the nation. At present it is calculated that every increase of 100,000 in the number of unemployed costs us £¼ million. It is also estimated that the Exchequer is losing £6 billion a year in reduced tax revenue and increased benefits, while another £10 billion a year is the cost of lost production to the economy and the nation as a whole.

But these costs to the nation are only the current price of unemployment and take no account of the long-term problems that are created. They do not include an estimate of the public expenditure over the years that will be made necessary by the need generated by present or even earlier levels of unemployment − for example, the social security costs of the long-term unemployed, who seem bound to spend many years out of work before they join the poorest ranks of the retired; the extra sickness and invalidity costs; the greater numbers going into mental hospitals or long-stay homes; and the greater need for residential care and other services that one might expect for those who retire early in poor health. In the United States there have been more attempts to calculate the long-term economic costs of higher unemployment as a result of the income lost due to higher rates of mortality, sickness and mental illness, and to the expenditure on additional prison and mental hospital admissions. It has been estimated for Britain that 'a sustained increase in unemployment of one million would give rise to additional public expenditure of £280 million on health and community services alone over a five year period' (Popay, 1981).

CHAPTER 7

Work for All

There can be no doubt that the massive electoral mandate given to the Conservatives in 1979 meant at least a tacit acquiescence in policies that would lead to increased unemployment. Subsequent surprise and indignation have stemmed from the scale and speed of increase without any reassuring sign that this is but a short sharp shock that will equally quickly set the economy to rights again. But in December 1980 there was little hard evidence that concern for what this has meant — in terms of higher and longer unemployment, more and greater poverty, and the simple erosion of lives as well as the frustration of hopes and ambitions — has gone more than media-deep. The needs of the young out of work and the 'new' unemployed — the redundant executives, the long-serving craftsmen and especially the 'three-month million-aires' of the steel industry — have received what attention there has been. These groups of course deserve support, but they seem to be getting it at the expense of the great majority of the unemployed, who tend to come from the lower-paid jobs and experience unemployment for longer and more frequently than most skilled or white-collar workers made redundant. Their families are most likely to experience poverty on benefits that the government itself has acknowledged are inadequate.

Political capital has of course been made out of the increased unemployment by the trade unions and by the Labour party, much more vigorously now that it is not in office. But so far, the sound and fury has signified very little in terms of constructive help for the unemployed or of proposals sufficiently positive and cogent to challenge and embarrass the current Conservative administration caught, in the words of a *Daily Telegraph* City columnist, 'more in an S-bend than a U-turn'. The TUC at last appears to be winding itself up for some constitutional changes to admit unemployed, but many trades councils warily keep their distance from unemployed workers' unions or even proposals for a centre for the local unemployed to meet and gain some mutual support.

The truth is that all governments, Labour and Conservative, over the last decade and a half have presided over major increases in unemployment on a scale that would have seemed impossible or intolerable in the 1950s when 'full employment' was so complacently assumed. Both parties are well aware that they cannot simply blame world conditions, the IMF, the multinational companies, the price of oil or the 'gnomes of Zurich' (whatever happened to them?). Other countries have faced similar economic problems without forcing the unemployed to pay such a price. Over at least the last ten years, every government has deliberately made use of some policies that they knew would increase unemployment whether to control inflation or the unions or both, or for any other reason. The unemployed have been used quite intentionally to solve Britain's economic and industrial problems. Yet throughout this period there has been not one major initiative to help those out of work to bear the cost of these policies and to compensate them for their loss. This inaction contrasts sharply with measures introduced in many other market economies.

Some speak of a return to the 1930s and a time of yet greater suffering and poverty among the unemployed. But why should this be? At least this time we cannot use the excuse of ignorance of the effect of unemployment on the lower-paid and the long out of work. In addition to the studies of the 1930s, which did not emerge till the depths had been reached of a greater recession than we have had so far, there is now more than sufficient evidence that policies of unemployment cause poverty and deprivation in Britain today. There can be no ignorance of this in official and government circles. The Manpower Services Commission, the Department of Employment, the Department of Health and Social Security and the late Supplementary Benefits Commission have all carried out and commissioned research and collected evidence on what unemployment means to families in poverty and the long out of work. This book has drawn heavily on their evidence as well as on independent research. A special Thinktank analysis of unemployment and its effects was also undertaken but, apparently, was not even circulated within the government. Yet neither party has introduced anything to help those who have to bear the heaviest burdens of unemployment. Instead many policy changes, some admittedly directed towards other groups rather than against the unemployed, have actually made the relative position of the long-term and poorer unemployed worse than it was before (see especially chapter 4).

Furthermore, the failure to compensate these unemployed for bearing privately the greatest costs of unemployment has been largely obscured by campaigns against 'scroungers', which have generally received tacit if not explicit encouragement from some ministers as well as many MPs. Meanwhile, unemployment is the main cause of increasing poverty. The rate of impoverishment is accelerating as the numbers of *very* long-term unemployed head past half a million. The rise will continue until well after overall unemployment has been falling for some time. But nobody is expecting that to happen yet, so poverty in unemployment will go on increasing in extent and intensity.

Maybe unemployment is necessary to combat inflation and many other ills. I happen not to believe that, but I am even less sure how we can justify the neglect of the increasing poverty that this policy brings. As a society we compensate many other victims of change, whether it is within the control of governments or not. The fact that unemployment is more concentrated among the lower paid, is likely to last longer and be more often accompanied by poverty than in some other countries would only seem to strengthen the case for more positive action and help, rather than further restrictions and cuts in benefits.

There cannot be a more legitimate object of the legislator's care than the interests of those who are thus sacrificed to the gains of their fellow citizens and of posterity.

This belief has long been a cornerstone of the most conservative arguments for social justice and was expressed in these words by John Stuart Mill long before the ideology of the 'welfare state'.

The failure of our present social security system to provide adequate help to the unemployed, especially those longer or more frequently out of work, has received wider recognition in recent years, although very many people still believe that the benefits are adequate and others are convinced that they discourage many unemployed from finding work. It is also pointed out that the poverty experienced in the last quarter of this century is not the same as that suffered in the 1930s. Equally, the poverty tellingly attacked by Charles Masterman (1909) in the first decade of this century was not the poverty of the 'hungry forties', the terrible mid-years of the nineteenth century. No doubt some of the many people who denied the hardships caused by unemployment in the 1930s made favourable comparisons with the years when Masterman described 'the prisoners' as he called the very poor or Jack London 'the people of the abyss' after his own experience, presenting himself as an out-of-work American seaman (1903).

The truth is that we do not yet have as detailed a picture as we have of the thirties of the depths of poverty to which many unemployed and their families are reduced today. Furthermore — just as in the thirties — the contemporary evidence is regarded sceptically by people who accept with little question the accounts of earlier poverty as a basis for their comparison — evidence which was rejected by many who were protected from the impact of the recession at that time. People experience poverty in relation to the rest of society at that time, not to others living a generation ago. They are deprived of what the great majority have come to expect. Social science and research seem to have advanced so little that society still appears unable to recognise poverty and suffering until it becomes documented by historians. Then we criticise previous governments and generations for their inhumanity and lack of will. At the time we seem only aware of the obstacles to doing anything, if we are not openly sceptical of the reality of the need to act. Today, as perhaps before, we also seem too preoccupied with what many see as impending disasters – this time massive technological unemployment – to be able to pause and recognise the impact of present and recent levels of unemployment. We do not recognise the need to meet the heavy costs which are already borne by very many unemployed and their families. To take up Elliot Liebow's comment again (see section 1.2), *they* are paying the price that we are told *we* as a country must pay to get the economy back on its feet.

In its final report the Supplementary Benefits Commission pointed out how easily the social security changes that cut the living standards of the unemployed had been accepted in 1980 – in great contrast to the uproar in the early and mid 1930s. The high level of inflation in recent years has concentrated people's attention more closely on what has been happening to their own standard of living.

Many changes in British society over the last generation have acted to widen social inequalities and so diminish people's ability to recognise and identify with the problems of some of the poorest groups in society. Unemployment has still not reached the terrible levels of the peaks of the inter-war years, but this is by no means the only reason. The growing hierarchy of state benefits has widened the different levels at which people are supported once they are out of work. Other developments in work and in the labour market mean that, despite the rise of unemployment, more groups have been able to achieve a certain security from unemployment for a greater part of their working lives – at least till now – leaving a vulnerable minority among the low-paid, self-employed and unemployed. The political and psychological significance of these changes are considerable and do much to explain the gap in living standards, contact and sympathy between the securely employed and the unemployed. Over the last decade in particular, a growing range of benefits well beyond the fringe have been added to the basic salaries and wages of those in the best-rewarded areas of work. This has helped to reinforce the gulf between the classes in the labour force and made membership of this privileged group of workers, or rather salaried earners, even more desirable. Other groups in work are now seeking or negotiating a share in these 'total remuneration packages' that may add another 30 or 40 per cent to employers' labour costs.

These developments have been fostered and encouraged by state activity ranging from fiscal permissiveness to legislation. Occupational pensions, private sickness benefits and medical care, company cars and private schooling for employees' children are just a few examples of the provision that has developed enormously in recent years. Not only does it provide extra status and reward for the recipient, it is one of the few growth areas amid increasing unemployment. As more people gain access to these benefits and services, their dependence on their job is increased by these 'golden chains'. To illustrate the creation of inequalities with two specific examples, a large proportion of the boats and yachts in one large south coast marina now belong to companies who use them to provide holidays for their staff and entertainment for business visitors. The cost to the company can with some care be set against corporation tax and the benefits to those who enjoy the trips are generally tax free. Secondly, there is an increasing number of firms, in London in particular, whose main business is to provide tailor-made suits for company executives. They are bought by the company at £200-300 and then, after a year or two, made over to the employee who is expected to declare their now-used value to the Inland Revenue. The resultant tax bill of perhaps £10 is the total cost to him of a new and expensive suit. To have increased the executive's salary to allow him enough after paying the usual rate of tax to go out and buy the suit would have been considerably more costly to both employer and employee. The result is a considerable tax subsidy to many of those with the highest pay and status, which of course reduces the public revenue available to meet the growing demands on public expenditure. It also makes it more difficult to reduce general taxation if 'tax planning' and 'tax mitigation' schemes continue to reduce tax revenue from those with higher incomes.

At the same time, the growing range of benefits that are gained by many groups in work increases their social distance from, and reduces their ability to identify with, those who remain unemployed or are caught in the trap of low pay and persistent insecurity. It may be that their additional security will no longer be adequate if we move more evidently from recession to slump and have to bear the brunt of the worst forecasts of the collapse of work in the micro-electronic revolution. People are starting to plan what we do to cope with this industrial Armageddon and the problems of the new unemployed. Yet we lack the will even to help those already unemployed: how high does the total have to rise before this changes? And even then, will the help be extended all the way down to those people many years out of work, or forced out of the labour force, and now subsisting deep in poverty?

People want and need the opportunity to contribute to the society in which they live: the right to a more generous and adequate benefit is not enough. To deny them the chance of contributing is to impoverish them by limiting their ability to participate in the daily routine of the majority and to share in the rewards that this brings. The main means of both contribution and participation for most people is work. The inequalities and inequities in the distribution of work and its reward are great in a class-ridden society − between those who are poorly and excessively paid, between those in fulfilling, absorbing and productive jobs and those in unsafe, insecure and appalling work, and between those in paid jobs and those in unpaid labour such as housework. But this does not weaken the argument for fighting unemployment as our first priority, as well as compensating those who suffer it more justly and distributing its cost more equally.

The 'unthinkable' that we should be planning for is not a society without work for many more than today. We should recognise that many more people want to work and contribute to the society in which they live than are able to. 'Why should we be concerned to persuade people that they will never work again when they want to work and their work is needed?' (TUSIU, 1980, p. 29). For this, as the workers at Lucas Aerospace have pointed out, is the other essential point. 'We have oversized classes when thousands of teachers are unemployed, old people dying of the cold when electricians and engineers are rotting in the dole queues, the biggest slump ever in the construction industry when seven million people live in slum or semi-slum conditions' (TUSIU, 1980, p. 29).

The amount of work that needs to be done is very considerable and includes much manufacturing and production. It is by no means confined to the currently much criticised social and personal services. But an urgent expansion of these too is needed to support and improve the quality of life of the growing number of people without wages including the disabled, the retired and the unemployed.

Instead we are cutting back on socially valuable work of all kinds. Local authorities have already been told to cut their spending on clearing the roads of snow and ice by 60 per cent this year. This will lead to more dangerous conditions on minor roads in particular, and presumably more accidents. The human costs may be considerable, but one might expect the most committed monetarist to reflect on the long-term health, insurance and other public expenditure costs of this immediate saving. British Rail will close 3,000 miles of track over the next decade if spending is not increased. Many train services will be cut, partly because rolling stock is not being replaced, and many stations closed or shut early to save labour costs (*Observer*, 30 November 1980). Yet this will limit the mobility of many older and poorer people who are dependent on public transport.

To propose work for all is not to enforce the work ethic, 'the idea that people must work and they must be persuaded to do so' (TUSIU, 1980, p. 29). The work ethic flourishes in a period of high unemployment, encouraging tougher measures against those out of work. More energy and concern is expended chasing those who take advantage of the lack of jobs than providing work for those who are desperately searching for it. Concern with work incentives and employ-ability causes unemployment to be seen as a personal problem and not a public issue: policies for the unemployed become reduced to a question of maintaining the will to work and this restricts the attention given to promoting welfare and providing proper compensation for those unable to find work. This helps to explain why we have been prepared to use unemployment in, for example, the battle against inflation and to relinquish so easily the objective of full employment. When asked what was the most important factor in putting a man on the moon, a German scientist replied: 'The will to do

it' (Grimes, 1979). None of the proponents of full employment or 'work for all' has claimed that it can be achieved
without effort and struggle. Beveridge in particular emphasised
the difficulties (see especially 1944, part V) and Kalecki
stressed the resistance there would be from those who would
lose some of their control and power (1943).

The functions that unemployment can serve in a capitalist
society were recognised by the proponents of full employment at the end of the Second World War. 'Unemployment is
politically dangerous. But it also serves to keep industrial
discipline.' The result is that 'there are still too many people
who . . . fear that full employment will jeopardise their own
freedom to do as they wish.' (Young and Prager, 1945, pp.
12 and 62). The political dangers have been much less than
anyone expected in the low unemployment years (Deacon,
1980b), so the attractions of unemployment as part of a
laissez-faire strategy have appeared all the greater. There has
been no pressure to find alternative strategies and so no will
to devote sufficient energy and resources to reducing its
extent. But unemployment deprives many people of their
freedom to do as they wish' (Young and Prager, 1945, pp.
the Full Employment Action Council has argued in the
United States (FEAC, n.d.), and the loss is borne by the
unemployed and by very many others throughout society.

The basic argument for 'work for all' is therefore a positive,
not a negative, one. We need to be prepared to make this case
and not allow the goal of full employment to become locked
into a vision of a dull, puritanical duty, symbolised perhaps
by the manipulative routine of 'Music While You Work'. We
need sustained full employment because it provides the
essential basis for many other policies: a more effective attack
on low pay and dirty jobs; positive programmes to counter
discrimination in work because of race, sex, age, disability,
hospital or prison record; and a strengthening of workers' and
citizens' rights to a healthy and safe environment in and out
of work. These depend for their achievement upon there
being more work to be done — *and* jobs available to do it —
than people looking for work. At present, the work to be
done is there, the workers are available, but the jobs are not.

This faces us with the challenge to examine in a much

more sustained way than ever before the relationship between the amount of work to be done and the number of workers that can be involved in this activity. We need to develop policies to provide work for all who want it including the 'silent reserve' of the discouraged and excluded outside the workforce (see section 1.1). Active employment policies must play a positive role. Rather than surviving to keep the younger unemployed 'off the streets', their basic objective should be to fit the supply of work to the demand for it. This should include a concern for the quality of work and its improvement: the aim should be a right to a career that provides satisfaction, not to work of any type, however ill-paid, insecure and demeaning. The very idea of equal opportunity to a career is in marked contrast to the fear that workers may refuse jobs because of social security benefits. No regard then is given to the quality of the job or the standard of living allowed by the benefits, or by low pay in work. The concept of job-ownership as a universal objective was beginning to receive more attention just as the days of low unemployment were beginning to disappear (see for example the Labour correspondent, *The Times*, 15 July 1966).

Today we are offered alternative scenarios with the growth of the informal economy, and the claim that this will help to break down the division between home and work, and unpaid and wage labour (for example, Gershuny and Pahl, 1980). The attraction of much work in the informal economy — the autonomy to control one's hours and length of work, the opportunities to find satisfaction — is important because it shows up the inadequacy of much offered in formal employment and challenges us to improve this. But at best it can only be a partial and inadequate substitute for 'work for all' that provides continuity, security and protection under law and the support of unions and professional associations. At worst it encourages greater tolerance of unemployment and sanctions tougher measures against the unemployed in the belief that they are enjoying all the possible benefits of work on the side.

There is also discussion of the greater opportunities for leisure in a society with less work, and this prospect too is attractive, given the long and unrewarding hours in many jobs and the lack of time to develop one's own interests. But there appears to be little interest in devising the means by which these opportunities may be equally shared so that all have access to the resources that are needed to take advantage of leisure, and all have the opportunity to contribute to and participate in society. In consequence, leisure becomes enforced inactivity for many with no means of enjoying the spare time. All too often it looks as if we are simply acquiescing in more premature retirement and more unemployment.

Whatever the amount of work available in society, we need to plan its distribution so that those who want work but are already treated as marginal do not become further excluded — dismissed as unemployable when we have no real interest in trying to find them work. If we are to avoid greater inequality in the distribution of work and so a heavier concentration of unemployment among the most vulnerable, we need to take account of the full range of needs and costs and not simply recognise the current distribution of power and the demands of those who have already established their position in the labour force. Only in this way can we make a more sustained attack upon the related problems of unemployment and low pay, two major causes of poverty in Britain today. This demands more active policies than existed in the low unemployment years. To develop the interest and resolve to plan for a society that involves all its members and actively promotes their participation in its work, we have to recognise more fully what unemployment means and how it affects not only those who are forced to waste substantial parts of their working lives but also the great majority of the population. Until we do, the heaviest costs are borne by many of the poorest members of society, and that whole society is diminished.

Bibliography

Data on unemployment and the labour force where no source is given are taken from the statistics published in the monthly *Employment Gazette* or in its predecessors, *Department of Employment Gazette, Employment and Productivity Gazette*, and *Ministry of Labour Gazette*.

Please note that London is the place of publication except where indicated and that all official papers are published by HMSO unless otherwise specified.

Allinson, Chris and Harrison, Jeremy (1975) *Youth Unemployment in Birmingham* (Young Volunteer Force Foundation).

Bakke, E. Wight (1933) *The Unemployed Man* (Nisbet).

Bakke, E. Wight (1960) 'The cycle of adjustment to unemployment' in Norman W. Bell and Ezra F. Vogel (eds) *A Modern Introduction to the Family* (Glencoe, Ill.: Free Press).

Barratt Brown, Michael, Coates, Ken, Fleet, Ken and Hughes, John (eds) (1978) *Full Employment* (Nottingham: Spokesman).

Beckerman, Wilfrid (ed.) (1979) *Slow Growth in Britain* (Oxford: Oxford University Press).

Berthoud, Richard (1979) *Unemployed Professionals and Executives* (Policy Studies Institute).

Beveridge, William H. (1909) *Unemployment: A Problem of Industry* (Longmans, Green).

Beveridge, William H. (1942) *Social Insurance and Allied Services* Cmd 6404.

Beveridge, William H. (1944) *Full Employment in a Free Society* (Allen and Unwin).

Bridge, Brian and Campling, Jo (1978) *Employment Problems — the social work involvement* (British Association of Social Workers).

Bulmer, Martin (ed.) (1978) *Mining and Social Change: Durham County in the Twentieth Century* (Croom Helm).

Caplovitz, David (1979) *Making Ends Meet: How Families Cope with Inflation and Recession* (Beverly Hills: Sage).

Carson, W.G. (1972) 'White-collar crime and the enforcement of factory legislation' in Eric Butterworth and David Weir (eds) *Social Problems of Modern Britain* (Fontana).

Clark, Marjory (1978) 'The unemployed on supplementary benefit'. *Journal of Social Policy* 7:4, October, pp. 385–410.

Colledge, Maureen and Bartholomew, Richard (1980) *Study of the Long-Term Unemployed*, Manpower Services Commission, February 1980. (Summary in *Employment Gazette*, January 1980, pp. 9–12)

Cooper, John C.B. (1980) 'Forecasting the UK economy: an overview' *Scottish Trade Union Review* no. 8, Winter, pp. 16–18.

Cooper, John C.B. (forthcoming) 'Forecasting the UK economy in 1981' *Scottish Trade Union Review*.

Cormack, R.J., Osborne, R.D., Thompson, W.T. (1980) *Into Work? Young School Leavers and the Structure of Opportunity in Belfast* (Belfast: Fair Employment Agency).

CPAG (Child Poverty Action Group) (1981). Forthcoming pamphlet on unemployment (CPAG).

CSE–LWG (Conference of Socialist Economists London Working Group) (1980) *The Alternative Economic Strategy* (CSE Books).

Daniel, W.W. (1974) *National Survey of the Unemployed* (Political and Economic Planning).

Daniel, W.W. and McIntosh, Neil (1972) *The Right to Manage?* (Political and Economic Planning).

Deacon, A. (1976) *In Search of the Scrounger* (Bell).

Deacon, A. (1978) 'The scrounging controversy'. *Social and Economic Administration* 12.

Deacon, A. (1980a) 'Spivs, drones and other scroungers'. *New Society* 28 February.

Deacon, A. (1980b) 'Unemployment and politics in Britain since 1945' in Showler and Sinfield (eds).

Dean, Andrew (1979) 'The labour market in a slow growing economy' in Beckerman (ed.).

Dex, Shirley (1979) 'A note on discrimination in employment and its effects on black youths'. *Journal of Social Policy* 8:3, July, pp. 357–69.

Dey, Ian (1979) 'A study of the formulation and implementation of policies relating to redundancy and unemployment by the AUEW district committee. Bristol 1970–72' University of Bristol PhD thesis.

Edelman, Murray (1964) *The Symbolic Uses of Politics* (Urbana: University of Illinois).

Edelman, Murray (1977) *Political Language: Words that Succeed and Policies that Fail* (New York: Academic Press).

Eisenberg, Philip and Lazarsfeld, Paul F. (1938) 'The psychological effects of unemployment'. *Psychological Bulletin* pp. 358–90.

FEAC (Full Employment Action Council) (n.d.) 'Full employment' leaflet (Washington, DC: FEAC, approx. 1977).

Field, Frank (ed.) (1977) *The Conscript Army: A Study of Britain's Unemployed* (Routledge and Kegan Paul).

Field, Frank (1979) *One in Eight: A Report on Britain's Poor* (Low Pay Unit Paper no. 28).

Finch, Janet and Groves, Dulcie (1980) 'Community care and the family: a case for equal opportunities?' *Journal of Social Policy* 9:4, October.

Forester, Tom (1978) 'The micro-electronic revolution'. *New Society* 9 November, pp. 330–2.

Gershuny, J.I. and Pahl, R.E. (1980) 'Britain in the decade of the three economies'. *New Society* 3 January, pp. 7–9.

GHS (annual reports) *General Household Survey* (Office of Population Censuses and Surveys).

Gould, Tony and Kenyon, Joe (1972) *Stories from the Dole Queue* (Temple Smith).

Gow, Lesley and McPherson, Andrew (eds) (1980) *Tell Them From Me: Scottish school leavers write about school and life afterwards* (Aberdeen: Aberdeen University Press).

Grimes, Alistair (1979) *Cold as Charity: Fuel Poverty in Scotland Today* (Edinburgh: Scottish Fuel Poverty Action Group).

Grover, Richard (1980) *Work and the Community* (Bedford Square Press).

Hamill, Lynne (1978) *Wives as Sole and Joint Breadwinners* (Government Economic Service Working Paper no. 13, Department of Health and Social Security).

Hannington, Wal (1936) *Unemployed Struggles 1919–36* (Lawrence and Wishart).

Harrington, Michael (1976) 'Full employment and social investment'. *Dissent* pp. 125–36.

Harrison, Richard (1976) 'The demoralising experience of prolonged unemployment'. *Department of Employment Gazette* 84, April, pp. 330–49 (summary of his report *The Effects of Prolonged Unemployment* Department of Employment).

Hartley, Jean F. (1978) 'An investigation of psychological aspects of managerial unemployment'. University of Manchester PhD thesis.

Hill, J.M. (1978) 'The psychological impact of unemployment'. *New Society* 19 January, pp. 118–20.

Hill, M.J. (1974) *Policies for the Unemployed: Help or Coercion?* (Child Poverty Action Group).

Hill, M.J. (1976) *The State, Administration and the Individual* (Fontana).

Hill, M.J. (1980a) *Understanding Social Policy* (Oxford: Blackwell).

Hill, M.J. (1980b) 'Unemployment and government manpower policy' in Showler and Sinfield (eds).

Hill, M.J., Harrison, R.M., Sargeant, A.V. and Talbot, V. (1973) *Men Out of Work* (Cambridge: Cambridge University Press).

House of Lords Select Committee on Unemployment (1979 and 1980) *Evidence* House of Lords Papers 144.

Into Work South London (1980) *Summary of Findings – September 1980* (Into Work) mimeo.

Jenkins, Clive and Sherman, Barrie (1979) *The Collapse of Work* (Eyre Methuen)

Jordan, David (1979) *A New Employment Programme for Disabled People* (Disability Alliance with Low Pay Unit).

Kalecki, M. (1943) 'Political aspects of full employment'. *Political Quarterly,* pp. 322–31.

Keating, Peter (ed.) (1976) *Into Unknown England 1866–1913* (Fontana)

Large, Peter (1980) 'So how do we fill the time in an Athens without slaves?' *The Guardian* 19 November.

Layard, Richard (1979) 'Have job centres increased long term unemployment?' *The Guardian* 5 November.

Levison, Andrew (1980) *The Full Employment Alternative* (New York: Coward, McCann and Geoghegan).

Levitan, Sar A. and Taggart, Robert (1976) 'Do our statistics measure the real labor market hardship?' American Statistical Association Annual Meeting, Boston, Mass.

Liebow, Elliot (1970) 'No man can live with the terrible knowledge that he is not needed'. *New York Times Magazine* 5 April.

Lindley, Robert M. (ed.) (1980) *Economic Change and Employment Policy* (Macmillan).

Lister, Ruth and Field, Frank (1978) *Wasted Labour* (Child Poverty Action Group).

London, Jack (1903) *The People of the Abyss* (New York, Macmillan).

LPU (Low Pay Unit) (1980) *Minimum Wages for Women* (LPU).

Mackenzie, Norman (ed.) (1958) *Conviction* (MacGibbon and Kee).

MacLeod, A.K. (1979) 'Recent redundancy studies – implications for manpower policy' in MSC (ed.) *Redundancy Studies and Implications for Manpower Policy* (Edinburgh: MSC Scotland).

Marsden, Dennis and Duff, Euan (1975) *Workers – some unemployed men and their families* (Harmondsworth, Middx: Penguin Books).

Masterman, C.F.G. (1909) *The Condition of England* (Methuen).

Mencher, Samuel (1968) *From Poor Law to Poverty Program* (Pittsburgh: University of Pittsburgh Press).

Metcalf, David (1980) 'Unemployment: history, incidence and prospects'. *Policy and Politics* 8:1 pp. 21–37.

Miller, Robert (1980) 'Who are the unemployed? – the irrelevant 1930s'. *Economic Affairs* October, pp. 56–7.

Minsky, Hyman P. (1965) 'The role of employment policy' in Margaret

S. Gordon (ed.) *Poverty in America* (San Francisco: Chandler).

Moylan, Sue and Davies, Bob (1980) 'The disadvantages of the unemployed'. *Employment Gazette* August, pp. 830–831.

Moylan, Sue and Davies, Bob (1981) 'The adaptability of the unemployed' *Employment Gazette*.

MSC – Manpower Services Commission (1980) *Manpower Review 1980* (Manpower Services Commission).

National Commission on Technology, Automation and Economic Progress (1966) *Technology and the American Economy* (Washington, DC: US Government Printing Office) vol. 1.

National Economic Development Council (1963) *Conditions Favourable to Faster Growth*.

NCU (Newcastle on Tyne Trades Council Centre for the Unemployed) (1980a) *Agitate, Educate, Organise* (Newcastle: NCU).

NCU (1980b) *On The Stones* (Newcastle:NCU).

Newcastle upon Tyne City Council (1980) *Redundancy in Newcastle upon Tyne: a case study* (Newcastle: Policy Studies Department).

North Tyneside Community Development Project (1978) *In and Out of Work* (Home Office).

OECD (1965) *The Requirements of Automated Jobs* (Paris: Organisation for Economic Co-operation and Development).

Pahl, R.E. (1978) 'Living without a job: how school leavers see the future' *New Society* 2 November, pp. 259–262.

Parker, Stanley (1980) *Older Workers and Retirement* (Office of Population Censuses and Surveys).

Phillips, D. (1973) 'Young and unemployed in a northern city' in D. Weir (ed.) *Men and Work in Modern Britain* (Fontana).

Piachaud, David (1980) 'Social security' in Nick Bosanquet and Peter Townsend (eds) *Labour and Equality* (Fabian Society).

Pilgrim Trust (1938) *Men Without Work* (Cambridge: Cambridge University Press).

Popay, Jennie (1981) 'Unemployment: A threat to public health' in CPAG.

Reubens, Beatrice G. (1970) *The Hard-to-Employ: European Programs* (New York: Columbia University Press).

Road, Alan (1980) 'A tale of two steel towns'. *The Observer Supplement* 7 September.

Robertson, G. (1979) *Housing Tenure and Labour Mobility in Scotland* (Edinburgh: Scottish Economic Planning Department).

Rose, Hilary (1973) 'Up against the welfare state: the claimants' unions' in Ralph Miliband and John Saville (eds) *The Socialist Register 1973* (London: Merlin).

Ryan, William (1971) *Blaming The Victim* (Orbach and Chambers).

SBC (Supplementary Benefits Commission) (1979) *Annual Report 1978* Cmnd 7725.

SBC (1980) *Annual Report 1979* Cmnd. 8033.

Scottish Economic Planning Department (1980) *Redundancies in Dundee* (Edinburgh: SEPD) Summary and Report.

Sennett, Richard and Cobb, Jonathan (1973) *The Hidden Injuries of Class* (New York: Vintage).

SHAC (Scottish Housing Advisory Committee) (1980) *Allocation and Transfer of Council Houses* (Edinburgh: Scottish Development Department).

Showler, Brian (1976) *The Public Employment Service* (Longmans).

Showler, Brian (1980) 'Political economy and unemployment' in Showler and Sinfield (eds).

Showler, Brian and Sinfield, Adrian (eds) (1980) *The Workless State* (Oxford: Martin Robertson).

Sinfield, Adrian (1968) *The Long-term Unemployed* (Paris: Organisation for Economic Co-operation and Development).

Sinfield, Adrian (1970) 'Poor and out of work in Shields' in Peter Townsend (ed.) *The Concept of Poverty* (Heinemann).

Sinfield, Adrian (1980) 'Unemployment in an unequal society' in Showler and Sinfield (eds).

Sinfield, Dorothy and Adrian (1968) 'Out of work in Syracuse and Shields' in Irwin J. Deutscher and Elizabeth J. Thompson (eds) *Among the People: Encounters with the Poor* (New York: Basic Books).

Slater, Robert (1975) 'Coping on the dole'. *New Society* 14 August, pp. 367–9.

Smee, Clive (1980) 'Unemployment and poverty: some comparisons with Canada and the United States'. Paper presented to the SSRC Research Workshop on Employment and Unemployment, June 1980.

Smith, David J. (1980) 'How unemployment makes the poor poorer'. *Policy Studies* 1:1, July, pp. 20–6.

Soothill, Keith (1974) *The Prisoner's Release: A Study of the Employment of Ex-Prisoners* (Allen and Unwin).

Soothill, Keith (forthcoming) 'Employing white-collar ex-offenders'. *British Journal of Social Work*.

Sorrentino, Constance (1980) 'Unemployment in international perspective' in Showler and Sinfield (eds).

Stern, Jon (1979) 'Who bears the burden of unemployment?' in Beckerman (ed.).

Stonier, T. (1979) 'Technological change and the future'. Paper presented to the British Association for the Advancement of Science Annual Meeting, September.

Titmuss, Richard M. (1958) *Essays on 'The Welfare State'* (Allen and Unwin).

Townsend, Peter (1979) *Poverty in the United Kingdom* (Allen Lane)

Trewsdale, Janet M. (1980) *A Report on Unemployment in Northern Ireland 1974–79* (Belfast: Northern Ireland Economic Council).

TUC (1980?) *Homeworking: A TUC Statement* (Trades Union Congress) undated.

TUC (1980) *Services for the Unemployed: Discussion Document* (Trades Union Congress) November.

TUSIU (North East Trade Union Studies Information Unit) (1980) *Life Without Wages* (Newcastle: TUSIU).

Walker, Alan (1981) 'The economic and social impact of unemployment: A case study of South Yorkshire'. *Political Quarterly* January.

Walker, Alan (forthcoming) 'Towards a political economy of old age'. *Ageing and Society*

Wedderburn, D. (1973) 'Working and not working' in D. Weir (ed.) *Men and Work in Modern Britain* (Fontana).

Young, Michael and Prager, Theodor (1945) *There's Work For All* (Nicholson and Watson).

Index

Active employment policy,
    147–157
age and unemployment, 63, 67,
    76–83, 123, 127
    poverty, 80–82
alternative economic strategy, 9
apprenticeships, 45, 71, 72, 80
army, 74

Benefits, *see* unemployment
    benefits and supplementary
    benefits
Beveridge, W. H., 128–130, 136
birthrate, 70

Cambridge Economic Policy
    Group, 15, 16, 145
class and unemployment, 57, 69,
    99, 151–153
Cohort Study, 20, 21, 43
    poverty and, 50, 51
Community Enterprise
    Programme (CEP), 101,
    104
comparative unemployment, 5,
    13–15, 16, 17
Conservative party and
    Conservative governments,
    9, 97, 114, 136, 142–145,
    147, 148; *see also*
    monetarism
"credentialism", 72, 73, 101,
    108

destocking, 12, 13
disabled people, 36, 38, 125–127
duration of unemployment, 25,
    42; *see also* long-term
    unemployment

Early retirement, 12, 77–79, 120
    illness and, 82
economic costs of unemployment,
    140–146
employers, 96
    redundancy and, 96
employment service, 97–106
equal opportunity, 85, 108,
    112, 122–127
executives, 18
experience of unemployment,
    18, 35–41, 90–93

Fair Employment Agency
    (Northern Ireland), 123
families,
    effect of unemployment on,
    53
    help finding jobs, 45, 46
female unemployment, *see*
    women
forecasts of unemployment,
    15–17
full employment, 1–6, 17, 119,
    127–132, 155–157
    policy of, 4
    regional variations and, 23, 24

Geographical variation in
    unemployment, 23—27

Housing, 30—34, 51, 52
    Scotland, in, 33

Illness and unemployment, 82;
    see also disabled people
    invalidity benefits, 109—111
incentives, 5, 154, 155
income maintenance, *see*
    unemployment benefit
    and supplementary
    benefit
inflation, 149—151
    pensions and, 81, 82
"informal" and "irregular"
    economy, 116, 117, 156
interventionism, 141, 142, 144
investment,
    industry, in, 142
    micro-electronics, in, 138
Ironbridge Museum, 99

Job centres and job shops, 44,
    46, 47
job release scheme, 101, 102

Labour force and labour
    market, 64, 84, 85,
    124—127, 129, 130, 141,
    142; *see also* Vacancies
Labour party and Labour
    governments, 17, 114,
    147, 148
leisure, 156, 157
long-term unemployment,
    89—96, 105, 116
    poverty and, 92; *see also*
    poverty
    regional variations in, 25
    United States, in, 90
looking for work, 41—47
low pay and unemployment,
    18—20

Manpower Services Commission,
    91, 97—99, 103, 137, 148,
    149
    forecasts by, 16
measurement of unemployment,
    generally, 7—9
    long-term, 89, 90
    overcount, 119
    undercount, 11—15
micro-electronics, 2, 79, 86, 127,
    133—139
monetarism, 2, 139, 143—145,
    154

National Front, 122
National Insurance, *see* unemploy-
    ment benefit and
    supplementary benefit
new towns, 28, 29
number, *see* measurement of
    unemployed

occupation and unemployment,
    18—23
older workers, *see* age and
    unemployment
organization of unemployed,
    47—49

Pilgrim Trust Study, 105
poverty, 20, 22, 49—57, 149
    age and, 80—83
    clothing, 51, 52, 113, 114
    defined, 54
    housing, 51
    long-term unemployment and,
    92
    Poor Law, 106
    resources, 50, 51
    women, 87, 88

Race and unemployment, 18, 47,
    75, 121—123
Rayner enquiry, 112
recession, 2, 10, 15, 50, 71, 140
redundancy, 58—68, 102, 113
    community, effect on, 64, 65
    labour market and, 64
    payments, 60—63, 107

unemployment distinguished, 67, 68

unions and, 66

registration, 11, 84

repeated unemployment, 21, 27, 28

resources of unemployed, 40, 50, 91, 92

retirement, early, *see* early retirement

Robbins, L., 130, 131

Search for work, 41–47

short-time working, 12

"silent reserve", 12, 123

skilled workers, 18–20, 42, 58

Special Employment Needs (SEN), 103, 104

Special Temporary Employment Programmes (STEPs), 101, 104

Supplementary Benefit and Supplementary Benefit Commissioners, *see* unemployment benefits and supplementary benefits

Sweden, 67, 97, 105, 125, 129, 130

Technological change, 133–139; *see also* micro-electronics

temporary employment schemes, 12, 102

third world, unemployment in, 2

trade unions, 48, 49, 66, 147, 148

"unemployables", 9, 13, 90, 91, 94, 157

unemployment benefits and supplementary benefits, 106–118

earnings-related supplement, 107

faults in system, 107, 108

inelegibility, 108, 109

insurance benefit, 107

invalidity benefits, 109–111

poverty and, 113, 114

supplementary benefits, 106, 111–114

Supplementary Benefits Commissioners, 107, 116, 148, 149

Unemployment Review Officers (UROs), 115, 116

United States,

comparative unemployment in, 5, 17

computers in, 134–136, 138

cost of unemployment in, 146

equal opportunities in, 123, 124

old people in, 79, 80

poverty in, 22

young workers in, 70, 71

Vacancies, 8, 10, 11, 89, 121, 122; *see also* Labour force and labour market

White-collar workers, 58

women,

micro-electronics and, 137–139

numbers working, 84

poverty, 87, 88

supplementary benefits, 108

unemployment, 21, 39, 83–89, 123

work ethic, 2, 3, 42, 154

workless state, 119–122

Youth, 2, 68–76, 123

Youth Opportunity Programme (YOP), 69, 74, 75, 98, 100, 101